# NEW VOICES

## Contemporary Writers Confronting the Holocaust

Edited by **HOWARD DEBS**
and **MATTHEW SILVERMAN**

VALLENTINE MITCHELL
LONDON • CHICAGO

*First published in 2023 by Vallentine Mitchell*

Catalyst House,
720 Centennial Court,
Centennial Park, Elstree WD6 3SY, UK

814 N. Franklin Street
Chicago, Illinois,
60610 USA

**www.vmbooks.com**

British Library Cataloguing in Publication Data:
An entry can be found on request

978 1 80371 026 6 Paper
978 1 80371 027 3 Ebook
978 1 8037 1028 0 Kindle

Library of Congress Cataloging in Publication Data:
An entry can be found on request

# Contents

## PART IV
## Aftermath  173

# Artist Statements

## About the Prelude Drawings

When I began my illustrations for this book, one word echoed in my head louder than any others: humanity. Humanity, during times when it feels most beautiful, humanity during times that seem to have none of it, humanity during times that don't even exist yet. With that word in mind, I wanted each of my drawings to contain not just symbolism from the Holocaust, but above all else, a deeply human element. Each drawing in *New Voices* contains a human base, and that is what I hope readers of this book resonate with most: that though the victims of this horrific event were people that they have never met, or may have no biological connection to, they could have been people who look and are like them.

My work was also inspired by the few drawings that survived out of the Jewish ghettos and concentration camps, impressions of a dark world often surreptitiously created during rare and dangerous moments. It didn't feel right to create work that was particularly representational, colorful, or beautified. I wanted to match the rawness of the original artists of the time, who dared to capture the moments that cameras missed. Additionally, I tried to remain sensitive to the subject matter in itself; as a young person learning about the Holocaust decades after it happened, I felt it is not my place to create direct visuals of the horrors that occurred. I instead tried to portray the darkness that these horrors left behind. It is an honor for my art to be shown alongside the work of the incredible contributors to this book, and what I learned as I created these drawings is what I hope readers take with them at this book's close: that though the Holocaust happened in a world that seems like it exists only in the past, crimes against humanity take place around us globally in a world that is very much the present.

We must not close our eyes to horrors happening in the world just because they are not right in front of us. They are happening every day. My hope is that the readers of *New Voices* feel transformed in some way by the time they finish reading it, enough that they, in turn, help change the world for the better.

*Rachel Futterman is a Graphic Designer and Illustrator living in New York City. She holds a BFA from the State University of New York at Oswego, and has been drawing for as long as she can remember. Outside of her full-time design job, Rachel continues her mission to create artwork that gets people thinking beyond the paper to see beauty in what is ordinary and unseen.*

## About the Cover Image

The cover image is from a portion of my poster "Symbols: The World Entire." During and prior to WWII Hitler's Nazi party used variations on the triangle to identity citizens and prisoners in concentration camps according to religion, ideology, sexual orientation and other distinctions. Some, but certainly not all of these symbols were; Yellow Star of David – Jews; Purple Triangle- Jehovah's Witnesses; Red Triangle – Political Prisonsers; Black Triangle- Asocials and Lesbians; Brown Triangle- Gypsies; Pink Triangle – Homosexuals; Blue Triangle – Emigres. Many prisoners wore a combination of symbols; there were also markings which designated repeat offenders, flight risks, country of origin, etc. The poster itself appears in Holocaust Museums internationally.

*Amy E. Bartell is an artist and activist who believes in the power of art as a tool for positive social change. Her work addresses issues of social justice and diversity and is distributed internationally through such venues as the Museum of Tolerance in Los Angeles, California and the United States Holocaust Memorial Museum in Washington, D.C. Her commissioned works include: The National Organization for Women, the National Gay and Lesbian Task Force, the Worcester Women's History Project, Vera House, The Q Center and for the Freedom to Marry Campaign. She has also created over two dozen murals on college campuses and for non-profit organizations including: SUNY Oswego, Syracuse University, Carleton College, California State, Wells College, Towson University, Monmouth University, The Food Bank of CNY, AIDS Community Resources, University of Connecticut, University of New Hampshire and Washington State University. She is the recipient of the Unsung Heroine Award from the National Organization for Women and the Rubenstein Social Justice Award from Syracuse University. She teaches illustration and graphic design; her studio is in Syracuse, NY.*

*A representative sampling of some of her work can be accessed at http://www.aeoriginals.com/ including "Symbols: The World Entire" which was made possible by Debbie and Al Gaynes in memory of her grandfather, Chaim Ariyeh Chasan, who perished in Vilna in October,1941.*

# Introduction

Nature and concept of book, why *New Voices?* / Purpose and
character of the book components / Contributors, their task, what
they bring to the task / Intentions, what we ask of the reader

Anna Ornstein in her pioneering work "Artistic Creativity and the Healing
Process" (see note in foreword for full citation) which clearly prefigures the
development of the nascent field of neuroaesthetics writes, "art ought to be
one of the most successful methods by which traumatic memories as well as
nontraumatic ones may be preserved and transmitted to future generations."

Janina Struk (*Photographing the Holocaust: Interpretations of the Evidence*)
writes: "Photographs are fragments. They illustrate stories, they do not tell
them." The premise of *New Voices* is to consider the "visual artifacts" presented
as "silent witnesses" of that time each to be given an interpretive voice for our
contemporary post-Holocaust world. *New Voices* juxtaposes these vintage
photos, propaganda posters, etc. selected from noted collections with newly
written work from writers (poets, short story, and flash fiction writers) additionally incorporating essays from scholars and specialists exploring key areas of
concern. Ultimately the book's intention is to memorialize, conceptualize, and
transfigure these "pieces" of the Holocaust through the literary arts and in the
process, universalize as well so as to focus on the moral lessons for all of
humanity. It is recognized that while also including many other groups, the
primary victims of the Holocaust were Jews, that the Holocaust was essentially
about the genocide of the Jews, that Nazi ideology was rooted in antisemitism.

The concept for the book takes as its impetus the idea of the late Rabbi
Jonathan Sacks (zt"l) which he calls "universalizing particularity." Applied to
the tales we tell, the approach is present from time immemorial, in lore and
the bible, the practice of griot and maggid.

*New Voices* will be considered an anthology, only because *New Voices* is a new thing without known precedent. The term "construction" better applies. There are four doors, these are the essays; there are forty-nine windows, these are the poems, there are nine rooms, these are the stories.

Delving into the research which brought about this project is not within the scope of this introduction. Suffice it to say that using the visuals approach has certain merit for both the writer and the reader; balancing poetry, story, and essay in one volume does as well. While each element has its own important impact, all the elements coalesce to hopefully produce an overall "experience."

*New Voices* calls upon a diversity of contributor voices of many different backgrounds, from many different places, because *New Voices* starts with the idea that recognizing diversity bears on what it truly means to be human, that this is but one of the lessons the Holocaust teaches. Each contributor starts from where they are from, figuratively and literally, and in "confronting" the visual with which they have been carefully matched, takes a journey which the reader is asked to join.

All those associated with *New Voices* appreciate the responsibility entailed and the potential pitfalls. In regard to the visual content for example—which is important since its inclusion is not incidental but integral—the position of Susan Gubar (*Poetry After Auschwitz*) must be considered, particularly aimed at the photography of the Nazis, which constitutes the bulk of the photographic record extant, she writes, "The visible not only hides the unseen and promulgates a morally problematic distancing but also generates factitious, duplicitous testimonies."

Indeed serious admonishments abound, from Adorno to Ozick. Finally, the raison d'être for *New Voices* stems from Elie Wiesel; in *Entre deux soleils, One Generation After* he writes, "Still the story had to be told. In spite of all risks, all possible misunderstandings."

The ultimate goal of *New Voices* is to keep the flame of memory and truth ignited.

# Foreword

**Confronting the Past, for the Sake of the Future:**
A Conversation with Anna Ornstein, Psychiatrist, Holocaust Survivor and Joy Ladin, Poet, Literary Scholar

(Note to the reader: The following has been edited for length and clarity. The complete unabridged conversation series may be accessed at newvoicesproject.org)

## PART ONE

**JL:** I was wondering if you had questions for me before we start?

**AO:** Yes, just one question. Was there anything special about this particular project that you volunteered to do this with me?

**JL:** There were several things. This idea, which I thought was very exciting, an opportunity to talk with you, and I'm very interested in your work, and I've done a series of conversations like this with people who are interesting, and I love that way of relating to people. Also, I feel that it makes ideas that might be abstract or dry; it gives them life and vitality. So, it was the kind of thing that I wanted to do in general. And, of course, I was thrilled to be able to do this with you.

There were two other reasons. I have a personal stake in this not in terms of my family; both sides of my family; as far as I know, most of them had emigrated in the first decades of the 20th century. They came to the United States or Canada. So I didn't grow up with any [...] people who had died during the war. But as an American Jew growing up in the 1960s, and 70s, American Jewish identity was taught to me as being rooted in a certain idea of the Holocaust where I and I think many of us were taught that the core of American Jewish identity, the core of what it meant to be a Jew, was to be alive after the Holocaust, which meant to turn Jewish identity into this negative thing that was rooted in horror and I grew up being taught that, you know, having survived the Holocaust, that's what made a really good person, going through the Holocaust, dying and or surviving.

1

My generation of course, could never aspire to be good in that kind of way. But the least we could do is continue to define ourselves in those ways. And I never liked this definition of Jewish identity. I have a deep connection with Judaism as a religious tradition. I know Jewish history is very long. There are lots of atrocities in there. There are also wonderful things in it. So even as a child, I was dissatisfied with this. And when I was in my 30s, I felt called upon to write a book [related to the Holocaust] in the voice of a woman; the book is called *The Book of Anna* coincidentally. So the last piece of it is that I was asked, when I was in my 20s and 30s, before or maybe when I was working on *The Book of Anna,* I don't remember the exact chronology, but I was invited to review a bunch of books about Holocaust poetry.

At that time, I had to think about what was I doing? What were we doing? What was the difference between doing it well, and doing it badly, or did any kind of poetry about the Holocaust work? And I knew that, yes, I had my own feelings about this. Remember, I grew up with the Holocaust being this thing. And I also grew up writing poetry. My parents weren't interested in my poetry, but if I told my mother that I had written a poem about the Holocaust, she would immediately start to tear up. And I thought, oh, wow, this is a very powerful thing. And yes, I was a child without ethics. And so I really enjoyed telling her that I was writing about the Holocaust, because it got this emotional reaction from her. But I just kept that feeling. What is this? Is that really what I'm doing if I write about the Holocaust or is there something that's worth doing?

There are three things that I'm hoping that we will talk about. And if we don't cover everything in this conversation, we can do it in other conversations. There are three big questions that relate to this book that I'm looking forward to talking with you about? One is arguments against artistic representation of the Holocaust. There are strong arguments. I've written about some of them myself, as you know, I've personally wrestled with them as a poet. Arguably, this is so sacred or so mysterious, or so unknowable that the better thing is not talk about it, or we have no business talking about it.

As near as I can tell, the objections come in several different varieties. They all relate to, stay away or you'll mess it up, basically, but there are different flavors of that. So one flavor of it says, this is unspeakable, that if you represent it in any way, you are misrepresenting it. And you're desecrating it. And the most sophisticated version of that would be kind of like what Maimonides[1] says about why we shouldn't talk about God, that human language always makes us feel like we know things when we don't, it puts things into categories, it suggests that there are similarities between things. And so some people say you can't put the Holocaust into language. Primo Levi[2] is one of the people who said this. He wrote very eloquently about his experiences in the camps, and then he killed himself. And one of the things that he said—

**AO:** It is questionable. His suicide is questionable.

**JL:** Oh, I didn't know that.

**AO:** Oh, definitely.

**JL:** That's good to know. I will look into more about that. But he wrote that the only people who really have any business talking about this are the people who died.

**AO:** Yes.

**JL:** So everybody else has varying degrees of you shouldn't be talking about it, because you weren't really there. It's kind of like the genocide version of if you remember Woodstock, you weren't really there. So, if you're alive, you can't really speak about the Holocaust because you weren't really there even if you were there and suffered through it if you were a survivor.

**AO:** I have immediately a response here.

**JL:** Please. What are you thinking?

**AO:** I am thinking all along, while I'm listening to you. Because what I hear, and this is already what I had been listening to and responding to that—then those of us who survived, I am a survivor, I think you know that, have no business being alive. There are experiences that are very very difficult to articulate. But we have nothing else but our voices to tell you a story that we are determined to tell about.

And I experienced this as one that would put us into the "we have to die because we have no business being alive." I don't want that future for myself, and coming back to the book itself, when [the editors] decided that they want to invite people to listen to the Holocaust in a new way, give it new voices, what they said was we are very much afraid that this story, the Holocaust, will suffer the fate of all historical events, eventually, they will be forgotten. That is how it happens. The motivation to write this book must have been, I think, I didn't discuss it with them, that they didn't want it known only in history books, that teachers find in a library, because that is the only place that event is noted, and all they know about it is it happened in the 20th century; it happened in Europe, period—there will be nothing, you know, and I have a very different view.

I think this book was created in order that the Holocaust not suffer this particular expected fate that all they will know about it will be a date and it will be in a book in some library that you have to search for. And they said maybe we can prolong the life of this event by having a new book with new voices. And that will help, to survive for another generation and for another one, I am sure. [...] you and I are engaged in the discussion of a book that was I would say, the brainchild of two people at least [the editors] who said, maybe if we find artists, that is poets or [fiction writers] who will associate to pictures that come from that period and now will be "heard" and interpreted in a new way—so they gave us the opportunity to listen to these new artists, that is, poets and [fiction writers] essayists too.

**JL:** And that's a beautifully eloquent response. So the two arguments against doing this that I gave you, those are the most extreme arguments, I would say, the absolutist arguments or the purist arguments, there are other arguments that relate to what you just said, that I'd like to just put out on the table. But to be fair I want to go backward, because we just [...] [commemorated] *Tisha B'Av*[3] and *Tisha B'Av*, the observance of it not only involves a fast, but it involves the reading of a poem about the horrors of that historical event. It is a first person rendition. It's in the voice of somebody who did not die, right.

So answering Primo Levi, it's somebody who didn't die in that event. We read it, and it was included in the Torah[4], for the very reasons that you said, which is that poetry has the capacity to make and to keep what would otherwise become history and feel like "that was then" and it's more and more general, to keep it fresh and keep us grounded in something of the sense of how it was lived. So there is a long precedent that supports what you were saying within Jewish tradition.

**AO:** I am just thinking that we Jews, maybe because we have so many incidents, so many events that we have to remember, they found a way of doing that, by making the event and its memory into a day of fasting.

**JL:** That's right.

**AO:** But then the question is, are we losing our way in which we used to remember?

**JL:** Can you say more about that? That's a profound question.

**AO:** I tell you interestingly, because I cannot write any more as I did, it came to me in terms of my own experiences, and that is I was thinking about the loss of the *Shabbat*. [Sabbath]. We should now, even at the time of that book, you know, by Heschel[5]—

**JL:** Oh, Heschel's book *The Sabbath*?

**AO:** Yes, and I was thinking, you know, this should really recognize [question] what does modern man know about the feelings, the meanings of having *Shabbat*—don't do anything that is the ordinary. Because I grew up in an Orthodox home. And it is natural, that once you go to the university and you have a practice [occupation] and you have children, what do you do with your day of *Shabbat*?

You need to cook because you're working otherwise or you go shopping because when else will you have time to do those things. So now, when you see *Tisha B'Av, I* am thinking about my father, and all the times that came before naturally. But I myself now, only one generation away, I don't even remember on the day on which it occurs. So, I don't know whether or not we Jews are going to join [some] other groups of people who don't really care about their important days that separated one day from another day.

**JL:** I think that you're raising—this is really a profound cluster of questions about the fact that well, as a poet, if I write a poem, I think of the effect of that poem, not that it's going to be part of the biblical canon, or people will celebrate holidays and read the poem. In other words, I think of it as something that individuals will read, if I'm lucky, and they'll have an experience.

So that is very different. It's a secular, modern, individualized, I would say, even capitalist way of thinking about artistic expression and what it can do. And as you're pointing out, that limits the very quality of memory and meaning that you can have [for] something like *Shabbat*, and I would say also the traditional *Tisha B'Av* observance, because they're communal, and I'm thinking of the two versions of the Ten Commandments in the *Torah*, one says, "keep" the *Shabbat* and the other says "remember" it.

And so it's the combination of remembering it and being in a community that does it [both] together that creates possibilities for kinds of memory, and kinds of experience that we certainly should be worried about losing; I haven't thought of this before. I'm freelancing here. You've stimulated new thinking, which I'm grateful for. So, I was going to point out that there were two more objections I'm going to propose.

One is, I think, important, but trivial compared to what we're talking about. So I'm going to [mention] it and then I think we can probably move on. One is that anything that you do in a capitalist society, you know, individual artists create things or, you know, publishers publish books; it has an element of profit, and some people have talked about "*Shoah*⁶ business." That this is a way that people can gain fame, gain publications, gain whatever it is, cultural esteem, that individuals can get. So that is one of the objections that this is—

**AO:** Like a business.

**JL:** Right. Because I will confess, I wish *The Book of Anna* had been a *New York Times* bestseller? Yes, I do. Of course I do. That's the culture that I grew up in. And that was the model of success. As a poet did I think that was the, you know, is that a good? You know, [in] relation to it? I wouldn't say so. But it's what my culture gives me for this endeavor. The more profound question though, and I'm thinking about [it] differently in relation to what you just said, is, if you read Lamentations, if you read *Eicha*,⁷ you notice that it uses highly conventionalized language, it uses the same images over and over again, not only that, but the images that it uses, you can find in the biblical curses that are in Deuteronomy, you can find them in other prophets, right?

The culture, the poetic culture of ancient Israel, as most poetic, traditional cultures are, it's not about innovation. It's about conventions, you have a bunch of phrases that mean [evoke] images that have deep meaning, and you put them together in different ways. So one of the more profound questions about Holocaust poetry is that it generates its own clichés, that it takes the events and puts them into words. And then those words become formulas. So in the ancient culture, in the sacred culture that *Eicha* comes out of and that still lives in some Jewish communities, you can say, that's right, that's the way this works. Right?

Prayers are conventional language that we give deep meaning to because it's sustained by a community. But one of the arguments against writing Holocaust poetry is you're just generating clichés. And so you're reducing, you're not adding to the ability to remember, you're not adding to the ability to talk and think about this. You're actually taking it away. Every time somebody writes a poem where there's the image of smoke from a gas chamber, the readers of that poem, say, oh, yeah, yeah, Holocaust—smoke from a gas chamber—I've heard it all before. And that feels like it relates to what you said about what is the capacity for memory that we have? And that we need? And are we losing the kind of memory that we need?

**AO:** Now Joy, let me ask you, with this, the very last image, smoke from the chimneys. Interestingly, for me, the image is helpful for the memory.

Maybe, because I actually had seen it. But I am grateful for the poet's ability to give it expression, so that you too can imagine the smoke. So why would we deprive ourselves of the possibility to articulate, to find the forms and [basis] of seeing something that brings it to you, your image, because it's not your memory, but now, you do have a picture of it? And at least you have that picture.

I [will] tell you, one of the things that I found very interesting: how are the very famous artists remembered? You take, not Cézanne, but the very famous [Modernist] painter—Picasso. Everybody who goes to a museum has seen Picasso. And it is interesting. I looked into [it]: what is the picture, the image that most people will remember, among the many, many hundreds and 1000s of pictures they had seen from Picasso. It will be *Guernica*[8] people remember. And then they remember that event that is commemorated by that picture. And you think, how come? People want to remember that story. And now they have an image that helps them remember. When they go to the museum they say, "Ah, this is Guernica. This is what happened there."

**JL:** I love the idea that you just articulated and correct me if I'm wrong, but it sounds like you're saying that images, both the visual, artistic images as opposed to like the photographs in *New Voices*, which I want to talk about [...] or going to Auschwitz right, so photographs or going to the location, that's giving yourself first person experience of some kind of how this looked, not how it felt or what it was like to live [be] there, but how it looked.

But artistic images, artistic representations, you're saying, have a different function for you, which is a poetic image or the painting like *Guernica* gives an artistic form that enables people in future generations and people who've lived through the events to be connected through this form to them—and that is actually what the poem Lamentations does, what *Eicha* does.

You know, it is true that it's a convention, that it says, you know, women eating their own children that they've just given birth to—when you read about the horrible sieges in the Iron Age, that's what they would do, they would starve people to that extent. But there is a way in which that image to this unimaginable level of horror and desperation continues somehow to bind the generations together.

**AO:** Yes. That's right. And I tell you, we are in a way, in our situation as Jews, because we are exposed to so many of these events that we also have the ability to articulate, with new voices, that we can find images, that the images can be now accompanied with new voices, and new people who read [like] Lamentations.

**JL:** Right—When I had my first child, and he was three, I think, when I was able to celebrate his first [Jewish] holidays. And so I was aware of these holidays in a new way. And first, there was *Purim*[9] and I thought, oh my God, this is a holiday that makes it fun to talk about genocide. And then I realized, I mean, I was like, oh my God, as a Jewish parent, I have to have a little fun holiday so my child learns how to deal with it if they try to kill you all, and then a month later, we have Passover[10], where there's another genocide that we're remembering. This one is, you know, another failed one, but not a failed one. 400 years of slavery, as African Americans will tell us is no picnic. Right? It's not the same as genocide. But it's a horrible thing to go through.

**AO:** I just want to say, you know, it's making me laugh a little bit, because I think that the Jews should celebrate every day, our ability to articulate that, that we have to remember.

**JL:** Yes.

**AO:** That we have the [basis] to do that. I happened to write a foreword to another book very recently, [related] to a group of people who don't have written language. Now, they only remember what they [are told] from their [elders] and maybe eventually it will be remembered, but [maybe] not. So there are cultures now in this world, many of them who don't have a written way of remembering [...]. We Jews, maybe [we] got it from the Arabs, [we] were not the first ones, we were so excited by the ability to write, we never stopped. [Find] a Jew and he will tell you a story and the story will be written down very quickly.

**JL:** That's right.

**AO:** And I'm glad for it and proud of it.

**JL:** That feels to me like a powerful rebuttal of the first two objections.

**AO:** Yes, I'm glad.

**JL:** And also, it sounds like you're saying that whatever the risks of represent-ation, it's a function of actually being alive and surviving. And it's something that we do because we don't only exist as individuals; I think that it is questionable if I, as an individual poet, say, oh, my career is going nowhere.

I know, I should write about the Holocaust, people will love that. That's an obscene thing to do. However, collectively, whatever the [...] motivations of the individual artists to engage in this—and there's nothing about being an artist that makes you a great human being or anything, we're all just as complicated and human as anyone else. But nonetheless, artists are the way our species does this together. Like we have to do it. Because being an artist, being a poet, means that you're in the business of creating these images and giving form to events and feelings. And you might be doing it for the worst reasons, you might not be doing it well, but nonetheless, it's still your job to do it as part of a people and as part of a species that requires this I would say to live.

When I was writing this article about what good Holocaust poetry might be like, right, this oxymoronic thing as a literary critic—like if you said to Picasso, alright, Pablo, we want you to paint a response to Guernica, the atrocity of Guernica. And he said, well, you know, how can you do that? That's just a horrific thing. There are photographs; just look at the photographs. I don't want to do anything to change the image, but what would make a good painting about Guernica?

And one of the things that is striking about that painting is that the horror in it is tied up with a language of images that is very, very hard to process. I've seen that painting many times. And I never remember it. I can't remember because the composition is designed to make it feel chaotic and to rupture the systems of meaning where, you know, [like] that beautiful one of Cézanne's apples or something like that. I remember the apple, it's lovely. I couldn't paint it. But you know, it's not like, I can't remember that a painting of an apple is a painting of an apple. But with *Guernica*, I literally can't remember what there is, I remember the feeling of it. But every time I see it, I have to process it anew.

**AO:** This is [it], this example is [perfect], very good. You know how long we've been talking?

Almost an hour, and I know that I would love to talk to you more. I [would] love to listen to you more.

**JL:** That feeling is mutual. I think we're [just] to the beginning of the other part of the conversation. So maybe [we need] another session where we can talk about how *New Voices* works, and we'll look at that sample poem together.

**AO:** Maybe [we should] be more [...] disciplined, and stick to the task.

**JL:** Well, I feel like what we just did really very well [we] talked about the pros and cons of this debate about artistic representation. So I feel like now we've sort of set the table for this. And where we've ended up with is [...] you and I were in agreement, that part of what art is doing is different from what photographs [alone] do. It's different from what visits to the sites of atrocities do because it's creating forms that have to be reassimilated by individuals, it is creating an event that happens inside [each person]. And so in our next conversation, I'm hoping that we can talk about [that] because I know you're an expert on this—

**AO:** I don't see myself expert in anything in particular,

**JL:** That's my favorite kind of expert—

**AO:** Maybe in child psychiatry I [am], not in art; I just enjoy it and try to understand it. But you know, my whole life was just writing very ordinary things, what happens to people [...] when they are not well, and mainly, I was working with families and children who had emotional problems. It was not art.

No, my job was not even related. It's interesting [about] that one article[11] that you may have seen, but that is really the only one in which I engage the issue of art. Because I am not an artist, but it is funny that, you know, most of these things go back to a story; I simply walked into a bookstore. And I saw a very large book. And it cost a lot of money, over $100, one book; we had so many books in our house the last thing I needed was another book.

But this was an amazing book; this book was a catalog that was prepared by one of the universities near Chicago. They had an exhibit of all the—you've probably seen that book—all the art that was created in connection with the Holocaust. And I didn't wait another minute, I bought that book right away. And that is where I learned quite a bit of why art became so important, even to the people who were incarcerated. Now I see how important it was and for what purpose. And maybe we should talk a little bit more about that, too.

**JL:** I think that that's important. And I just want to say I admire the essay that you wrote greatly. And I, as a poet, I felt like you understood very deeply the different impulses to make art in circumstances of excruciating suffering.

**AO:** Did you ever, did you visit Auschwitz?

**JL:** No, I haven't.

**AO:** [Well] if in case you ever do, you will be surprised. There is a museum in Auschwitz. You [perhaps] heard about that. And that in itself is an amazing story and how [it] happened that there was a museum; there was a person who was found painting a horse, but he was not allowed to paint anything other than what he was told to paint, painting that horse was a no-no.

And they took him to the head person in Auschwitz. And they thought he will be killed, right on the spot for doing something that he was not supposed to do. That was the punishment in a place like Auschwitz you know. In any case, this man was not a Jewish man; I think he was a political prisoner. And to save his life, he made up a story, a very clever one. He said, you know, sir, what we need here for our officers, we need a museum, we should [have one] yes, why not?

And there were all these people who were making all kinds of pieces; I would love to tell you more about it, how I learned about what that museum was, and what it became. Now, if you ever go to Auschwitz, you can see that museum because there is one and people say, What? a museum in Auschwitz—yes.

**JL:** It is really extraordinary that on the one hand, you have the prisoners, for whom making art was a way of maintaining humanity and surviving that was a survival and resistance strategy. But you also had the people who are working there who were in a very different way [...] being dehumanized and needing, maybe not deserving, but needing art also, as a way of remaining in touch with their humanity.

**AO:** Exactly. you know what Joy we do have to stop simply because if it is left up to our need to talk, like the women who were in the same cell in the *Gefängnis* [concentration camp]—I say certain things in German. Do you speak German?

**JL:** No, I don't.

## PART TWO

**JL:** So Anna, I am grateful for our discussion of the general arguments surrounding artistic representation, and memorialization of the Holocaust. And I feel that you have not only endorsed the idea that this is something that's permissible to do contrary to some of the arguments that it's immoral or destructive in different ways, but that there is a real obligation and need—which are two different things—so that [...] Jews or, I think American Jews, are raised feeling there's a communal obligation to remember the Holocaust and it sounds like you feel that artistic representation is part of fulfilling that obligation.

But also, apart from Jewish communal sense of obligation, that there is a human need to create these representations to enable us to do what it seems like are two different kinds of things. One is to keep memory alive. But the other is to create present day experiences that connect the present and the future to what's happened in the past. So not just recording, writing it down, looking at photographs of it, but actually creating as *Guernica* creates new experiences whereby individuals confront different elements and are challenged to synthesize them in different ways—and in the act of that synthesis this goes from being somebody else's past to being something that happens inside each of us in the present. Was that right?

**AO:** Beautifully put, really beautifully put. [I just want to respond] to you beyond that. What went through my mind as I was listening to you—what happened to the idea that was so important in Jewish tradition, that we [were] not supposed to have representation? Certainly not anything related to God, or any experiences [of that kind]. That was forbidden was it not in the Jewish tradition? When the State of Israel was established, and we were going to [a] beautiful town in northern Israel, and there were artists all over [...]. And I asked myself, that was not supposed to occur in a Jewish culture. That was forbidden. And so I don't have the knowledge, but I wish I would know what happened [...] you're not supposed to do anything in God's image.

**JL:** So yes [...] it's interesting, if you look at the three Hebrew bible-based religious traditions—

**AO:** Yes, please.

**JL:** Right. So if you look at Christianity [...] what we think of as a prohibition against idolatry becomes actually just a prohibition against representation of what we would now call pagan deities, [...] so that is much laxer than Jewish tradition.

If you look at Islamic tradition, there is a much stronger prohibition, you know, iconoclastic strain so [...] that's the development of mosaic arts, but there was never a prohibition against artistic representations in Judaism. As you can see, when they excavate ancient synagogues from a couple of thousand years ago in Israel, they often have mosaic floors that represent animals and other things.

The prohibition in the *Torah* is against representations of God that are visible representations of God. But even as that prohibition is being given, it's given in the form of a narrative representation of God. So we read the story of Mount Sinai, that [...] sets the scene very vividly

[including] God, a mountain, fire and lightning and speaks with a voice and says, you know, don't represent me in terms of anything that you can see. So it's clear as that's being given that this prohibition is not, [it] does not apply to narrative—

**AO:** You see you just explained something to me that I should have asked before [...] with the establishment of the state [of Israel] in my own mind there was an increase [in art] [...] it was now okay to have images of the sort that I knew as a little girl, as a Jewish child, that we were not supposed to have those images. That maybe, the biblical period, in Jewish tradition, the biblical time, had introduced so many prohibitions that were not true for the ancient Jewish times. I think that we grew up—you grew up with the idea that you should remember the Holocaust—but I grew up with the idea that I was to know about Moses, but not necessarily to have a real idea of what he may have looked like.

**JL:** Very interesting. I know that when you [...] go to a museum exhibition of *haggadot* [booklets used for the Passover *seder*, i.e. service] from different times and places, many are illustrated in ways that I sometimes find surprising, but there are illustrations that include pictures of Moses and pictures of the plagues. Sometimes the pictures are in [incorporated with] the letters. So it's a fusion of the emphasis in the *Torah* on the word and written word and [...] it fuses that with pictures, [...] these beautiful—I don't even know what you would call it—my wife would know because she is a rare books curator, but yes, there's [...] a pretty wide range of Jewish visual practices, even though in general, [...] the visual arts had not flourished in Jewish communities the way that they have flourished in Christianity.

**AO:** Yes, [that is the point]. I just want to be very sure that we [...] complete our thoughts related to the book [...] I want to be sure that we stay with that [...]. So I wonder if we should now be more specific about continuing the conversation related to what the book contains, and why I happened to choose that image [as an example to talk about] of the little boy [...] there is a great deal in that [...] Here it is [image shown] [look at that] gorgeous face.

Now, we know he is a Jewish child, but we don't have the religion of the teddy bear. But as we learn from *New Voices*, now that the division is made in the culture, in the society, in relation to everybody, because the Jewish laws [Nuremberg Laws, enacted in 1935] have been instituted.

And this little boy—if he is [...] of a Jewish family, a mother and the father, his chance of surviving the next few years is very unlikely, as a Jewish child, who knows, he may go to the United States and survive. However, if he remains in Europe, his chance of survival is practically nil, very very little. And what happens to the teddy bear? [perhaps] he will be recruited in the SS [...] where he becomes the killer of the Jewish child [...]. Depending very much on where this child is [...] he may have the opportunity to emigrate with his family.

However, if he remains in Europe, he will be killed. He will be dead by the time this *dichter*—I speak German now [this poet writes] this verse [...] I am sorry. I get very very emotional because we lost one and a half million of these beautiful [...] Jewish children and that is what will happen to him. By the time the new poem is written, this child is no longer alive. He was not allowed to grow up. [...] he is killed by his own teddy bear. His teddy bear is going to be the one who declares that "you are a subhuman, you are not a human, they will build a factory in which the likes of you will be killed."

And that is the story that *New Voices* is going to tell us about, how that happened—that for twelve years after the time when Hitler came to power [until] the end of this horrendous time, one and a half million Jewish children were killed. And this story will have to be told, and you and I now have nothing [...] but to give this introduction to the story, that other generations will learn about this event. I am laughing because I am afraid that we cannot say it will never happen again. Chances are that now that we have learned this skill of killing people in masses, we will not give it up. [...] maybe I should not [say any more about this]. [...] I wonder whether you would like to [...] offer [...] another point that you would like us to relate to, together in a conversation about the way in which this terrible crime was committed over [so many] terrible years?

**JL:** Thank you. [...] You said so much. And I do this to my students also, they say—so many things come out. And then I get in the way and I go back and I say okay, let's take things one at a time, I want to make sure that we really think through them.

But I want to start with the last two things you said and then go back to talk about the way *New Voices* works and how this photograph is working, because you demonstrated many different ways that it's functioning. First *New Voices* includes different kinds of elements; that includes photographs, it includes captions of photographs, [...] which are two separate things. [...] there's a [separation] [...] between the photographs and the caption. So you often don't know [the details of] what the pictures are [about].

You go from the pictures to usually a poem that responds to the pictures, sometimes a story that responds to the pictures, sometimes prose that's not fiction or poetry that reflects, as you're reflecting now, on larger issues or questions about how did this happen? Why did this happen? How does it relate to the present? So there are many different elements. And I always tell my poetry students, that if you want to communicate information, poetry is a very poor choice of medium. And I think photographs also are a poor choice of medium. So [...] probably Homer would disagree with me, would say, you know, actually it worked pretty well with the *Iliad*, conveying history through poetry, but really in general, I think that there are more efficient ways of considering large questions of what happened in what order and how did this happen and sociological analysis of the sort that you're asking for.

And while *New Voices* includes some of those materials, it foregrounds instead, this very, I guess, montage of different elements that do not efficiently communicate chunks of information or chunks of perspective about these events, but that instead ask us to relate the different elements and meditate on them and think about them in new kinds of ways. Ultimately, I think that it is adding up to—I don't know if you know the Woody Allen movie, *Hannah and Her Sisters*—

**AO:** I remember seeing it, [...] I know I have seen almost all of [his movies].

**JL:** There's a bitter European artist living in New York, played by Max von Sydow the great actor. And he's sitting at home watching television and his much younger girlfriend comes home and says, "what were you doing" and he says, "channel surfing." He's like, you know, he's trashing American culture, on this channel there was this, and on that channel there was that, and he said, "on one channel, there are these intellectuals saying, how about the Holocaust? How did it happen?" He said, "they can never answer the question because they're asking the wrong question. The question isn't, how did it happen? It's why doesn't it happen more often?"

And I think that what you're saying about the human taste for genocide, I think that there is some [...] evidence, although it's not at all conclusive, that there may have been genocide between [...] different early human species, Neanderthal and Cro-Magnon in some places, although [...] there were other kinds of interactions, but there is a way in which genocide does seem to be part of the human potential. And that is balanced against this very specific, very modern, industrialized, industrial scale, institutionalization of genocide, which does [seem] new and shocking. [Let's look at] the picture [again], because [...] Anna you had a series of very illuminating and deep responses to this picture.

So I just wanted to tell you what I was hearing. One response was that you looked at it, and you said, we see a beautiful child, and a teddy bear. And the image doesn't give us any information about what the Nazis would call the race of the child. But because [...] of the context that the picture is in and because it's in *New Voices* in the context of [...] these responses to the Holocaust, we know that that's the era it comes from, and then just as when Americans look at a picture of a child, they immediately look at the skin color and say, "Well, what race is the child?" I can't interpret this picture In America unless I know about the race, you're pointing [out] that once we know that this is a picture of a child [...] during the Holocaust, we immediately say to ourselves, is this a Jewish child? Or is it not a Jewish child? And [...] as soon as we ask that question, as you said, the picture becomes not just a picture of one moment in time, which every picture is, but it becomes a picture of multiple possible futures for this child.

**AO:** Exactly.

**JL:** Yes. So you said he could survive, he could go to America, he could stay in Europe, in which case his chances of survival are very small. There's the question of what happens to the teddy bear because once the teddy bear isn't with the child, it ceases to become a Jewish teddy bear. Right? And if we imagine him not as a Jewish child that would multiply other kinds of future so I thought that that was a very fascinating and profound response to look at one instant of time and to see multiple possible futures in the starkest sense being captured in this picture of one instant.

**AO:** Now, [...] I am continuing to be a teacher and making sure that [...] we've gotten as much [out] of this as possible, because there was just one reference that you made [...] in your comments that you actually use the word genocide [...] And because what this picture now tells us, in its "small" version, just what they see here—but in the "larger" picture we would know that that experience of what happened in the Holocaust was just one of the genocides of that one century.

So you think of the [...] one other genocide, the Armenian in the First World War, but after the Holocaust, we had a whole group following, [...] And I don't have to name them all because you probably have all of them in your mind. And so, we all know—we also have to think—what did the Holocaust tell us about human survival in this century, as we now can look back on it. We had I remember, in my own lifetime—and that is why I thought maybe my own experiences and my own memories would be sufficient to add [to the] foreword—because I am so old that I can remember so many of the actual events that [occurred]—you probably weren't yet alive, when already after the Holocaust we had a whole group of incidents, [in which] mass murder was committed. And maybe, as I said, maybe this is the teacher in me.

But I would say, when I'm looking at this little boy, and I see what his future may be, I have to think about all the other children of [...] Bosnia and Rwanda—and there is probably no end [...] this child represented the future of many children.

**JL:** Yes.

**AO:** [...] and these were not even as you would have said, legitimate wars, these were simply one religion—not only religious—I'm thinking about Northern Ireland and England and all the others; that is what consumed so much of human life rather than, instead of paying attention to what to create [for the good of humankind] we with our "big brain," we ended up creating [...] destructive items like the "big bomb" that now has to be "carried" from one president to the other. So, it is very difficult to think about the Holocaust without recognizing that that may have been only the greatest and most horrendous expression of a whole century that was almost as if it had been dedicated to destruction rather than to [...] life. I am so sorry, I sound terribly pessimistic, but I am not pessimistic, but this is what I learned from my life, because I have seen it very close [up].

**JL:** There's an Israeli poet, Dan Pagis—

**AO:** Yes, Pagis.

**JL:** —who grew up in Bukovina [Romania] and [in] short, he was resettled in Israel after the war; his parents were killed. He grew up in the camps; he learned Hebrew and immediately started writing poems. And one of the earliest was called "Autobiography." And he says, "I died with the first blow and was buried/ [among the rocks of] the field."

And as the poem goes on, you realize he makes it explicit, that he is Abel, and that his brother, he is Cain, and Pagis' way of representing what has happened to him is just like yours; although even in a broader perspective, he said, yeah, right at the very beginning of human history, you have this act of extermination. And that's the human family, one of the things that he does is he keeps—he doesn't allow himself in reflecting on this to project outward onto one group—oh, that's a German problem, that's a Rwandan problem.

For him, it's always, it's part of the legacy of that first family where there are only four human beings on earth. Two of them are brothers, and one of the brothers kills the other brother; that to him is part of the essential DNA really of the human race. Not all of it, but an essential part of it. But I also want to emphasize that part of the way that you were talking— [let's bring] the picture back up again, because one of the things that Anna is doing is teaching us to read these photographs. [...] in general, photographs are metonymic [...] [that is] we know that they're just a piece of reality, actually I had to learn to understand that.

But now we look at this photograph, and we don't say, oh, my goodness, there was a world that was just contained to, you know, a bear and a child, and it was floating around in the universe—we don't say that we say that this is one piece of a larger world. And we don't say that this moment existed outside of time, we say this moment was a moment in contemporary history. That's a metonym, this is a part that represents a whole, that points us toward a whole; you pointed out that this [use of] metonymy points to different possible futures.

And then just now what you said is this is also a metonym for all of the children who are in genocidal or pre-genocidal circumstances. And so, this is a part that represents that kind of a whole. And when we see it that way, then as you said, I don't think it's so much about optimism or pessimism, but it's just that we have to look at this child and say, right, the children whose lives are contiguous with yours; they're alive today. And they're going to be alive in 20 years, there are always going to be children who are in this state where their childhoods are targeted in this kind of way, where their futures are split in these terrible [...] possibilities, all of which, including survivor possibility include terrible loss and dislocation, and wounding.

And I am noticing that the author—we can see the title of the poem that comes after it [the photograph]—says "4 Views" and it's almost like she [the author] and you were seeing this the same way. She's seen one picture. And she says, well, I can't only have—I can't only present one interpretation of this picture. I have to respond to it by presenting multiple interpretations just as you have. I'm sorry, I interrupted you though.

**AO:** No, no, no, I was just thinking that—what I was thinking was, because there are all these ways of killing each other, like the [Cain and Abel example]—it is for that very reason that we have to be so clever [in terms of] really learning the ways in which we can give meaning to our lives [...]— Where does it say in the *Torah*, your job is to choose life?

**JL:** Actually the elderly Moses who is about to die, he is the one who says [it], right before he goes up the mountain for the last time.

**AO:** Yes, that's Moses that says that; because if that is what is in our "genetic" makeup, that eventually we will do these terrible things to each other, then [...] our job is indeed, to be very creative [about this] in every way we can possibly be.

**JL:** Yes. And I'm so glad that you brought that quote into this because I think one of the—I don't know if this is just an American problem—I think most people, when they're allowed to live their own lives, we just focus on our own lives. I mean, that's [like] when soldiers go off to war, a lot of times what they're fighting for, is just to be able to go back home and have a life where they don't have to worry about big things.

But when we do that, we sort of assume that life is the default choice all the time. And that is what makes us vulnerable to genocide and other horrors; Moses, at the end of his life, he's looking at this new generation; they're older than this child, but they're the children of the slaves [and] the slaves are all dead. These are the children of the slaves and their children, and they're about to go into the land. And Moses has actually given the first recorded [command] to commit genocide. He said, when you get into the land, remember, kill everybody, destroy everything and so, Moses—there's an irony that I didn't think of until just now—when Moses says, I set before you life and death, therefore choose life, Moses knows, don't take this for granted. Don't think that just by going about your business, you're choosing life.

That's not what human beings do. Human beings think they're choosing life, and they're actually choosing death. But he's also telling them choose to kill other people, you know, before and after that he's given this other kind of [command]. And it's clear that this entanglement of the highest levels of human consciousness, with the most terrible ways of construing collective identity— the way of construing collective identity that says I can't be me unless I kill everybody who's you? Right? That's the genocidal construction. Moses is at the same time saying, be a people that actively, consciously always chooses life, and also [it seems] be a people that remembers that the nations that are there, you have to get rid of all of them, otherwise, you can't be here at the same time.

**AO:** So do we [want to address] another question, or do you have to leave?

**JL:** I do unfortunately have to go. But I wanted to summarize that I think, in this [part of our] conversation, you've really shown us—not the theoretical reason, well, why include pictures in a book like this? you're showing that they're not there as illustrations, right? They're not there as factual documents, the way you would have pictures at a trial of a crime [...], you're showing that they're there because these pictures of the past provoke us to have very, very complex responses in the future.

And although we didn't get to talk about it this time—I'm hoping that we will—the book makes sure that we remember that, because you can imagine—readers do anything they want to with books; authors always imagine that we can force readers to do things. The truth is readers do whatever they want with a book. Teachers know that right? Students don't read things just because you tell them to. So some people may just flip through the pictures. But the book doesn't allow this to become a book of pictures because it keeps interrupting that.

Right after the pictures, there's always a complex textual response. And they're all very different. But they all are responses; every time I read one of them, I would then feel like I had to keep going back as I'm reading the poem or the story—you have to keep going back to the picture and saying, well, wait a second, you're responding in this way. What is it you're responding to now?

[...] going forward in the book is sending me backward to the picture. So even if I was lazy, and I didn't respond in the complex ways you did, now I'm being prompted to respond in those ways.

And even in the cases—because sometimes I'm like, no, I don't see the picture the way this author seems to have. Even that kind of a response forces me to be more personally involved in responding to the picture, which is to say, to take something that I might have just accepted as a piece of the past and [...] make it part of my present, because if I say, no, no, I disagree—okay, I've now created my own interpretation that's part of my present life going forward, rather than just a passive idea of, oh yes, I'm seeing this, I'm seeing that.

## PART THREE

**JL:** I notice that the subtitle of *New Voices* is *Contemporary Writers Confronting the Holocaust*. It doesn't say Contemporary Jewish Writers or American Writers or European Writers, it's presenting itself— [the group of writers as well as] the group it is speaking [to] are [...] people who are alive now, and presumably, that's the intended audience. But when I think about [say] the Civil War—and the way that I learned it in American history, which was not very good—It was very much as something that was over. It was a one-time event, right? We teach in American history, we talk about the Civil War, [...] as Americans should remember it—because there are countries that have civil wars rather frequently, or certainly more than once.

It's not something that a country can only go through once. But we always talk about it as though it was a unique [singular] event. It's long over, it's completely behind us. And while individual artists might choose to do something about the Civil War, [...] maybe they write a play, or they write a story, or they write a poem [...] I don't know of any books [...] that say *New Voices: Contemporary Writers Confront the Civil War*, you know, where they present everybody with images and say, write a response to these images. So, again, a unique historical event, it's located in a specific place, and it's in a specific time, and, yet, we don't remember it [...] in the way that [*New Voices*] is striving to remember [or think about the Holocaust].

And so I'm thinking, like, let's imagine that I'm [a] person [that has] graduated from college. I'm going into graduate school; I'm going to be some kind of an educator, or some kind of a leader. And I want to learn about how to speak about, think about, and remember, the Holocaust. I see this book, and I notice that you're in the foreword, you're mentioned in the foreword, I happen to be lucky enough to know you. And I say, Anna, can you tell me what you think I'll learn about teaching or remembering or thinking about or talking about the Holocaust from reading this book? What will I get from it that I won't get from other things?

**AO:** I would suggest that the idea that the editors had in mind, namely, that all that look at this event with "new voices"—that could be [done] every 10 years. [...] This book then would become one in which we are [asked] to find the "new voices," not [only] in 20 something [2020s] but 30 something [2030s] and 40 something [2040s] and that kind of "survival" of an historical event would be a remarkable thing. [...] you get the idea?

**JL:** So one thing, it sounds like you would say to me, one thing that I could get out of reading this book is actually a model [...] that I could transmit to my students. I could use this as a model of ways to keep engagement with the Holocaust alive, to keep it in the present.

**AO:** Right.

**JL:** Because I could give it to my classes. And I could say, we'll take a look at this pairing of a text and a photograph. Now, you try to do a response to this photograph and this text. And so that means that it could become not just one book for one time, but actually a step in a process that keeps going, am I getting that right?

**AO:** I [have] another idea that interferes with [...] [that], which is whether or not we will survive our own future. I don't know whether you'll get it. The idea here is that [...] this book, at this time in our lives, could be a model for "new voices." But there is an assumption that we as the people, the human race, [...] [that we] will survive our own future. We cannot say [...] and we don't know that. And that is not very [pleasant to talk about].

**JL:** Well, it leads to the next couple of questions that I wanted to ask you. One is, [...] you've now lived a very long time. So you've seen a lot of different ways that people have talked about the Holocaust, written about the Holocaust, you've gone to events, you yourself were mentioning that you go to schools and talk to children [about the Holocaust]. So you have seen over time and from many different angles, the afterlife, if I can call it that, of the Holocaust.

And so it occurs to me that there are several things, different things you might think; one thing you might think is, this is like the book of Ecclesiastes, you know Ecclesiastes?

**AO:** I don't know, you tell me about that.

**JL:** Ah, so King Solomon at the end of his life, he's very old and he says, "Vanity of vanities, all is vanity." Actually [literally] in Hebrew, it's "empty breath." It's all empty breath. I've seen it all. I've done it all. I've had it all. I've enjoyed it all. And frankly, it amounts to nothing.

And he says over and over again. Honestly, people keep doing the same things. The fool and the wise men, they all end up in the same place. [...] To me, it reminded me of my grandfather, actually. But it's absolute despair of human possibility. So you might say, I have heard it all. I've seen it all, human beings have learned nothing from the Holocaust.

You might say, and I don't think you would, that human beings have really absorbed all of the important lessons about the Holocaust and we have acted accordingly or you might say something in between. You might say, well, we have learned some things. But there are other things that we have yet to learn. And so I'm wondering what you would say and if it's a mix of what we have and haven't learned, if you could just mention some of the specific things that we have and haven't learned.

**AO:** Yes, it's a very, very [good] question. I would say that it takes me back to my own profession. And that is psychology, psychoanalysis and all that. Could you repeat that?

**JL:** Yes, if you think that we have learned somethings from the Holocaust. There are other things that we need to learn that we haven't, what are some of those things?

**AO:** Yes, and that is where I am stuck. And that is where we are. [...] We have not learned to avoid hatred. We have not learned not to retaliate when we are hurt or angry. We know a great deal about this particular [matter]; I wrote in my professional papers—I was focused completely on this idea of retaliation, when you feel that you were hurt, that can be [...] in terms of [individual] human beings, or a nation; [...] after the First World War, we [...] had to have a second one, because [of] retaliation.

So if [...] human beings could avoid that pitfall, that once they were hurt, because it will happen, it will always happen, that they—and this is the lesson that I would think humankind could learn, not to retaliate, because the need to retaliate, once you hurt, is what keeps this thing going. Because you were hurt, now you hurt the next guy, the next guy, and there you go. And I would say, maybe when we are all done, I would recommend [to] you one of my papers about this question of how [...] a human being can learn not to retaliate when they were hurt, [...] or as a nation, because that cycle is what repeats itself in individual lives, in families and among nations. I want to give you an amazing example of that. The Bosnian War, you remember—

**JL:** I was thinking of that as you were talking—

**AO:** When you take the war in Bosnia, [the] people were told, you have to remember that the Serbs were defeated. That was [some] 600 years before that they were in Kosovo. 600 years before [there was] a war that the Serbs lost. Now, [the people were told] you should retaliate for that war, and this is kind of the notion that [leads to these kinds of conflicts] [...].

**JL:** So you're in a way offering [this example], you know, the Bosnian War; I was thinking about that as you were talking and I was thinking about the way this idea of collective narcissism—where you can build a collective identity on this hurt, this sense of victimization and a sense of loss. And this is what binds [people] together.

**AO:** Yes, correct.

**JL:** Well, that is [also] a model of keeping the memory of something terrible alive. Right? So we're talking about how do we keep the memory of the Holocaust alive? One answer would obviously be well, let's just follow the example of, well there's the Serbs, they did a great job of it. We can also follow the example of the Nazis who built in a national German identity around the loss [...] in World War One, the sense of betrayal, somebody must have done this to us. There are many examples where peoples say what binds us together is the belief that other people have wronged us and as you say, we need to retaliate because our own sense of self is wounded.

**AO:** Correct.

**JL:** —In a way that we can never fulfill. I'm guessing that you don't want us to learn that lesson from the Holocaust, that that's not the way to keep that memory alive.

**AO:** Actually, what we want to do is learn not to retaliate, you know, and that is interesting. I didn't think of it [...] when the Jews—I was among them, I was very much alive and very much aware of what was going on [at the time]. There was no [sense of] retaliation [in that instance]. At that point, the Jews said [...] we are not here to retaliate. We want to build, but that [caused] some pain to the people who were living on that land [Palestine at that time] that we said we need to get back because we are stateless.

And we are entitled—oh, my dear husband, he felt so entitled, I wasn't so sure. I thought there will be a problem with that. And we did, we had several wars, because the Arabs thought [...] we have no right to come to this land. But I would say coming back [to the] [...] core cause to that, maybe we can acknowledge our own situation, and only justify it by the fact that we had no place to go. And the world around us even accepted that, otherwise, I remember—Oh, I remember so well—when the [multinational conference, 1938] [...] got together to [decide] where would the Jews go?

You know, Evian, it's a French town, that they gathered [in] together. And no country wanted the Jews. They didn't want any [Jews] we needed a piece of land, we had to have something. And I remember the discussion, even Australia [which] was practically empty, hardly any people in Australia living [there] at [that] time. But they didn't want any Jews. We were not welcome. We were stateless, homeless. And then [Israel] became a country that is now [...] [being]compared to South Africa. [...] And that is not in our "genes," [as Jews], not in mine. I [deplore] it when the Jews become so righteous. [...]

**JL:** So one of the lessons of the Holocaust is that [...] being victims [...] in one situation doesn't immunize you against being unjust in other situations. And another thing that I'm thinking as you're talking, [...] is that in *New Voices*, all right, it's got a whole lot of different things in it. But if it succeeds, in its parts, or as a whole, in keeping the memory of the Holocaust alive, does it keep that memory alive in a way that promotes this kind of collective narcissism and sense of victimization, which I certainly grew up with when I was taught about the Holocaust.

I was told I should feel that way. Jews were entitled, we were morally immunized because we had been victims in the Holocaust. Everything we did was justified, right? [...] this goes along with that retaliatory thing, that's on the spectrum, it's not the same thing. So if I read *New Voices*, or if I give it to my students and they read it and the memory of the Holocaust comes alive for them. [...] Does it come alive in a way that promotes retaliation, victimization, entitlement? Or is it brought to life in a way that promotes other responses, responses that are better responses from your perspective as a psychoanalyst?

**AO:** I say that the best response, and this is now the question, whether or not it is humanly possible to refrain from retaliation—and if we take the situation [of] what I lived through in terms of the war, the end of the war, and then the establishment of the state [of Israel] —The only thing we can say, and this is something kind of spiritual and I am not [...], I am too realistic. I feel that the only way would have been [if] people around [the Jews] would [have refrained] from retaliation. [...] And it's difficult for you maybe to follow because I wasn't clear about it. [...] when we are [...] saying, what can you learn from the Holocaust, you would say, you wish we could now learn that the Jews were entitled for a piece of land because they didn't have a home?

That the nations all around them would say, yes, let's get together and find that piece of land. The only problem with that will be that there will be no emotional contact with that piece of land. You remember, that was really the discussion about Madagascar and the other possibilities— [...] this is really the original way that the idea of a two state solution was proposed [...]. Because then you would say, yes, you have that right, [going back some] 2000 years, but only if you are willing to share it with the people who are living there. [...] you remember what [actually] happened, then all the Arab states came to destroy the country [...] But the idea of a two [state] solution may be would have been the one [...]

**JL:** [...] So it sounds like you're saying a couple of things we could or should learn from the Holocaust are, number one, over the course of history, terrible things are going to happen. Peoples are going to suffer; injustice will be done. That's a normal thing. And so just as individual people, that might be your clients, you would say, yes, you're suffering terribly, and suffering is part of life. [...] One of the things about being human is we have to learn to live with pain, you have to learn to live with suffering.

There are dysfunctional ways to respond to it, and there are better ways to respond to it, but we're not going to escape pain and peoples as a whole are not going to escape historical pain. So that's one thing. Another thing is that it sounds like you're saying—which is in a way, yes obviously this should be a lesson—I'm not really sure we've gotten it, but you're saying that, I know that people who were living in Palestine and the other Arab states, they were like, [reacting in terms of] this is a European problem. Why is the solution to where the Jews that you tried to exterminate should go—why is it to come here [...] to where we're living, but in a way, what you're saying is that one of the lessons that humanity needs to learn is that when people are displaced, become refugees, are subject to terrible injustice, which is happening now with the Rohingya, in Burma, it's happening with some people in Eritrea, there is a refugee crisis—

**AO:** Exactly. I know.

**JL:** And that, there is a responsibility of the nations of the world, to find homes and places for people. And that that is hard to do justly, it's hard to do in a way that doesn't create further problems, but that's what we need to aspire to.

**AO:** So what I am saying is that the "new voices" may not give us the perfect solution, but they're "livable" human solutions.

**JL:** Yes. And this gets back to that picture of the little boy and the [teddy] bear. And the question [...], what's the religion of the [teddy] bear? And what's the religion of the boy? And you said, well, this boy really represents children now, children throughout the ages, who are in this situation of being the focus of genocidal efforts. And the [teddy] bear in a certain way represents the way cultures—in the way that we single out and define things—right, so when this is the [teddy] bear of a Jewish child—

**AO:** Yes—

**JL:** It has one meaning in Nazi Germany, right, it's a Jewish [teddy] bear. But if you separate the bear and the child as the poem imagines, the bear can go along and become the bear of a Christian child, the bear of a Nazi child, the bear of somebody who has nothing to do with this, and it can go outside this social situation that's defined by genocide. So in a way, it's an image of this arbitrary definition of identity that is mobilized in genocidal situations, right?

**AO:** Correct, totally arbitrary. Yes, and at the end, we just have to say, I go back to my idea that the only thing we can do is to curb our need [which] in many ways [...] is anti-social, the need to, you know, go to different political ways in which people try to solve this problem. If you are not going to curb your own appetite [...] to take more land, or more money, [...] then we have to find ways; in other words there was communism, there were all kinds of efforts made to curb people's appetite. Unfortunately, [it] ends up coming back [to the realization] that you cannot curb [this] human appetite. And when you are looking for something—and this is the answer to the question, what does the Holocaust teach us? That at the end, this appetite means that you eat yourself up. Because what happened to Germany because of their appetite to have all of Europe and all of Russia [...], that they destroyed themselves in that process. And that would be a good lesson to learn.

**JL:** Yes. I want to say that I like that very much. But I feel that something [...]—I think that for, you know, there's no universal education for anything, [...] but for people who have learned about the Holocaust and one of the things that we have learned is that there is such a thing as genocide; the word 'genocide' had to be invented after the Holocaust, [and] the response to the Holocaust; and once you invent the word genocide, then [...] you're saying you don't need a word if something only happens once you just point at it, just say, that thing that happened there and then. If you say genocide, and if you create a law, laws that govern genocide, and a concept of human rights that governs genocide, you're saying, Yeah, we know that this is something people do. We have laws against theft, because we know theft is going to happen over and over again, speaking of appetite.

**AO:** Correct.

**JL:** So one thing I think we have learned is yes, this is something that people do. I think another thing that we've learned is that it's something that can become the way a culture defines itself. And this relates to what you said about the self-destructiveness of it. Right? So a whole culture can define itself in terms of this collective sense of wrong and hurt and need to retaliate.

And that becomes an appetite for endless violence that is ultimately self-consuming, because you can't ever heal a historical hurt. You can learn to live with it, you can accept it. As Jews, I think, in the best cases do with the Holocaust. We don't say let's hunt down Germans and kill them, we say, we have to live with this pain. [...] And one thing that I am struck by *New Voices* doing very powerfully, is the choice to take these pictures from different moments in the Holocaust. The pictures themselves, almost all of them, are utterly ordinary.

In fact, this was one of the things that I said in my feedback, sometimes without the captions [...] most of them without the captions, I would have no idea where or when this was. Here's a meeting with a group of people if there's no caption telling me it's Nazis, you know, I don't know it's Nazis; here, distinguished looking old white guys, they happen to be Nazi leaders, but if they weren't, they could be today's, you know, American leaders somewhere.

So one of the things that this format does is it says when you are living in the present, your reality is going to look the same way. Whether or not your culture has become a genocidal culture. You're going to have leaders having meetings. You're going to have rallies of people shouting and getting enthusiastic. You're going to have children sitting in—in an apartment with a toy, looking at a toy being happy; you'll have people who are in prison, you'll have people who are miserable, you'll have all of the ingredients—you'll look around, and reality will look just pretty much the way reality does.

But part of what *New Voices* I think keeps teaching me is that I need to keep asking. I need to not be lulled into saying, oh yeah, right, leaders are meeting, people are cheering, right, everything is fine, the world is going on just fine, children have toys, I need to remember that those very same things can be going on, when my culture has plunged into genocide, has dedicated [itself], is in a process which is going to lead to these enormously destructive and self-destructive appetites and rampages.

**AO:** So true. I think the project has a future. And people will look at it and say, I read a lot of ambivalence. At the end of it, it will not be a clear cut. And as long as it's human beings who are populating the world, it will be ambivalence and not clear cut. And the only thing we can do, and we have to do it very well [is to] recognize the danger of hatred, and therefore, keep love in big amounts. In other words, we have to be very much aware that that is in our nature, greed, possession and destructiveness. And the only answer to that is that [which] is the opposite. [...] not to make [ourselves] into people who can only kill and want to get more.

**JL:** Yes, that's right. [...] W.H. Auden in his poem that he wrote "September 1, 1939" so that was—there were many beginnings to the Holocaust, but that was one of them. [...]

**AO:** That was the beginning of the war.

**JL:** Right. And [...] he had spent a lot of time in Germany a few years before—Berlin was a very good place to be as a young gay man, very cosmopolitan. There are all kinds of people that the Nazis would later very soon destroy, but he had very warm feelings for German people. He didn't think that the Germans were uniquely evil. And so in this poem he's looking at this, and he knows what's coming. And he says: "I and the public know/What all school-children learn,/Those to whom evil is done/Do evil in return."

And what you're saying is the most important lesson of the Holocaust, and ideally a lesson that *New Voices* will help bring into the present, is that we all have to learn to respond to the evil that's done to us in other ways, otherwise, we're part of this endless cycle.

**AO:** Exactly. That would be a wonderful lesson.

## Notes

1   Maimonides was a Jewish philosopher and scholar of the Middle Ages.
2   Primo Levi was an Italian Jewish chemist, partisan, Holocaust survivor and writer.
3   *Tisha B'Av* is an annual fast day in Judaism, on which a number of disasters in Jewish history occurred, primarily the destruction of both Solomon's Temple by the Neo-Babylonian Empire and the Second Temple by the Roman Empire in Jerusalem.
4   *Torah* has a range of meanings, most specifically, the first five books of the Hebrew Bible (Pentateuch or Five Books of Moses).
5   Abraham Joshua Heschel was a Polish-born American rabbi and one of the leading Jewish theologians and Jewish philosophers of the 20th century.
6   *Shoah* is Hebrew for "catastrophe" often used to refer to the Holocaust.
7   *Eicha.* Lamentations begins with the Hebrew word *Eicha* (how), and the book is known in Hebrew as *Megillat Eicha* (the scroll of *Eicha*) and is read during the observance of *Tisha B'Av.*
8   *Guernica.* Painting done by Picasso in 1937 following the bombing by Nazi Germany and Fascist Italy at the request of the Spanish Nationalists of Guernica, a city in Spain's Basque region.
9   *Purim* is a Jewish holiday which commemorates the saving of the Jewish people from Haman, an Achaemenid Persian Empire official who was planning to kill all the Jews in the empire, as recounted in the Book of Esther ("*Megillat Esther*" in Hebrew; usually dated to the 5th century BCE).

10 Passover ("Pesach" in Hebrew) is the Jewish holiday commemorating the liberation from slavery in Egypt and the "passing over" or the sparing of the firstborn of the Israelites.
11 Anna Ornstein M.D. (2006) "Artistic Creativity and the Healing Process", *Psychoanalytic Inquiry*, 26:3, 386–406.

# PART I

# The Rise of Nazism and Heightening Antisemitism

## Prelude to Part I

Jewish Life in the 1930s / Beer Hall Putsch / Propaganda / Hitler Youth / Book Burning / Early Reaction/Resistance /Berlin Olympics / Jewish Boycott/Freedom Restrictions / Early Escape / Kindertransport / MS St. Louis Voyage / Kristallnacht

# Chanukah: Kiel, Germany
## YEHOSHUA NOVEMBER

On the sill of the Posner family apartment—
what else but a menorah?
And since this is late 1932, the window opens
to a view of—what else but?—a Nazi flag
hanging from the town hall's gray stones
on the opposite side of the street.
Akiva, his wife Rachel, their three children—
Gitta, Shulamit, Avraham Chaim—

absent from the photograph Rachel has snapped.
When darkness arrives, they will
step into the frame

---

**About the Photo:** Hanukkah candelabrum in the house of Rabbi Akiva and Rachel (nee Wuerzburg) Posner on Hanukkah; Kiel, Schleswig-Holstein, Germany, 1932.

to kindle the flames. The candles' symbolism almost too
obvious. The juxtaposition to the Swastika
almost cliché. But this isn't literature. This isn't
speculation. That a Jew walks down streets,
cooks dinner, reads the paper, sends letters

is remarkable given she is a member
of an eternal people. And here
is the eight-branched mitzvah object on the eighth night,
the precise physical proportions, the blessings—
governed by finite rabbinic rules
to draw the Infinite G-d into this shoe box
of a world. Like soul into body.
And note the couple's names:

The husband's that of the famous martyr
whose flesh Romans combed from his body.
The wife's that of the martyr's wife, who spent 24 years
of her marriage alone so he could study the secrets
stored in the crowns of letters floating like ash
from the scrolls Roman officers set aflame. This is 1932.
In four months, on the night following the boycott,

Akiva Posner will risk his life to provide Jewish burial for the body
of a young man who'd returned home for a visit,
shot as he crossed the threshold
of his parents' store. And the word for world—*Olam*—
is rooted in the word *Helem*,
which means the concealment of G-d.
And the number eight is one higher
than nature, one beyond the world
created in seven days. But we still have not found out
what six million means.

# The Child, the Bears, the War: 4 Views

JANE YOLEN

### 1. Jewish Child with Teddy Bear, Poland 1935

The caption *is* the story.
We already know everything about this child.
But Teddy Bear's' religion is not noted.
Perhaps in this country bears go to church
not synagogue, drink holy wine
with a cracker on his tongue.
Perhaps he will not be shot upon arrival
or sent into an oven, where his dark hair burns
with a peculiar smell, his eyes become pools.
Perhaps TB will be given a brown shirt,

---

**About the Photo:** Franz Lieberman with his teddy bears. Circa 1933–1935. the only child of Hans (a surgeon) and Lotte Liebermann, born January 19, 1929, Gleiwitz, Germany (now Poland).[1]

black boots, a black gun.
He will join groups
of other church-going bears
marching in perfect cadence.
The child, already noted,
and delivered to eternity,
with Little Bear in his arms
is a mere checkmark on a ledger,
without a name, only a number,
disappearing out of his story
into history.
Is he Franz, David, Mordechai, Joel?
TB no longer remembers him,
the playroom, the window, the phone,
the chair where they sang silly songs,
laughed at jokes no one else found funny.
TB's oven only bakes bread
and little cakes cut with crosses.
They are sweet and delicious, like lies.
He eats them up, and sleeps
as a human child sleeps.


## 2. That Boy

That boy is a Jew, but who would know
without the caption. Perhaps he is really
German, Russian, Polish, Irish.
Maybe he is Scottish, Italian, Greek.
He plays with two bears,
one big, one little, missing
only Mama Bear who might
have been the one to warn them,
the one to carry the child
on her broad shoulders
out of danger.

That phone, its dial. I remember
the ring tones, always comforting.
Papa calling about coming home,
or Mrs. Sheffield, across the hall,

wanting a play date with her daughter.
Or the butcher to tell Mama
her order was ready.
Not the Commandant instructing you
to line up, take off your clothes,
march into the shower room,
where it only, ever, rains death.


## 3. I Know This Child

I know this child, that window,
so like my own growing up.
From my bedroom I could see
into the neighbor's apartment,
The Greek lady who kept cats.
I was allowed to visit the cats on Sundays.

I know that telephone
which I was not allowed to touch.
It brought news to Mama
from Daddy who was off winning the war.
or Uncle Irv or Uncle Jerry, or cousin Bill,
also doing their part.

I know those bears, the big one especially,
though I preferred dolls with long hair
wearing the kinds of dresses I wanted,
in soft blues or bright yellows
and straw hats with ribbons
I would have had a closetful.

I know that boy, the one whose parents
brought him over, through the war
each carrying one straw bag
crammed with everything they needed.
And all he brought, he told me in second grade,
was one Big Bear, one Little Bear.

He carried the rest of it in his *kop,*
he said, pointing to his head,
his eyes wide and deep as pools.
"Speak American," I hissed at him.
When he burst into tears, I was surprised.
"I thought I was," he whispered back.


## 4. Only A Photograph

It is only a photograph, Daddy,
and you weeping like a boy
whose feelings have been hurt,
Like a girl with a skinned knee.
I could call the doctor on the phone
if you would let me dial it.
Here, hold Little Bear,
he keeps away the brown shirts,
the ones who took away your Mama,
your baby brother, with the wide eyes,
deep like the pools you swam in
when you were off with Uncle Sid.

But you have me, now. And Mommy.
And the new baby coming.
We are your family instead.
Enough is enough, Mama says.
Why are you crying, Daddy?
Is it the photograph again,
the boy with the two bears
who never made it out of the house?
Who died in the bombings or the camps
or the fire, or the ovens, those changing stories,
when no one came as you always come
to find me and take me home again.


## Note

1    In 1938 with the help of a cousin they received an affidavit that allowed them to be placed on a
     waiting list for visas. In June 1938 Hans left for the U.S. Lotte and Franz remained behind, then
     left Germany less than a month before Kristallnacht "The Night of Broken Glass."

# Imagining my Great-Grandfather before He Was a Partisan, before He Was a Father

JULIA KOLCHINSKY DASBACH

Perhaps, like them, he sat
feet wrapped or sinking into sand,
mouth full of waiting, hands

stained our people's sacred texts.
But no, not by the synagogue steps,
perhaps, like them, he sat

only beside a river, where even Jewish,
he could blend with Ukrainian birch,
mouth full of waiting, hands

---

**About the Photo:** Sitting on the synagogue steps, Czechoslovakia 1936.

transforming bark to body, leaving
shadowed prints for us to find.
Perhaps, like them, he sat

not knowing it would end, or knowing
far too well how forests fall,
mouths full of waiting, hands

unable to keep up
with all the bones or names.
Perhaps, like them, he sat,
a mouthful of waiting hands.

# The Beer Hall Putsch

TONY BARNSTONE

A pistol shot into the ceiling, storm
troopers surround the hall, and Hitler shouts,
*The revolution's come!* It's taking form
like the white froth of faces tossed about

upon a darkened broth of coats and dresses,
faces upturned to listen to the speaker
who claims they've been diluted, and addresses
how to make a stouter brew:

*The weaker racial seeds will be plowed and harrowed, earth*
*thrown on their heads, their faces drinking in*
*the rains of heaven. And if they rebirth*
*like plants, we'll cut their legs off at the shin*

---

**About the Photo:** A large crowd gathers in front of the Rathaus to hear the exhortations of a Nazi orator [possibly Julius Streicher] during the "Beer Hall Putsch." November 9, 1923.[1]

*and tie them up and serve them barbarously*
*with pitchforks to the heart and knives to chop*
*them skin from bone. We'll soak the spirit free*
*in yeast and boiling water, add in hops,*
*make Germany into a purer brew.*
*All we need is you, and you, and you.*

## Note

1    In 1923 the leaders of the German Combat Front and the NSDAP, led by General Erich von Ludendorff and Adolf Hitler respectively, attempted to overthrow the government of Bavaria as the first step toward the establishment of a nationalist regime in Germany. On November 8, a meeting was held in the Buergerbraukeller in Munich where, after a speech by Adolf Hitler, the putschists called for a march on Berlin. The next day General Ludendorff led the rebels on a march through Munich to the Feldherrnhalle. There, police broke up the march, killing sixteen people and wounding many more, including Hermann Goering. Adolf Hitler fled the scene but was captured two days later at the home of his comrade, Ernst Hanfstaengel. Prominent pro-Nazi government officials withdrew their support, and the putsch was quickly put down by the German army. Hitler and other captured putschists were tried and convicted of treason. While Hitler was imprisoned in Landsberg, he wrote his political manifesto, Mein Kampf. Upon his release in 1925, Hitler resumed leadership of the Nazi Party.

## Postcard, 1932

DAN BELLM

Oh—
I see there is nowhere here
to stand—

broken cross,
iron fist,
the tyrant's hard stare

---

**About the Photo:** Propaganda postcard showing a crowd of saluting Germans superimposed on an enlarged image of Hitler and a Nazi stormtrooper. Circa 1932.

into a future
we're not meant
to live in—

emblems of
worship that have
started

appearing
in the streets,
on our walls,

many—
armed crowd
marching as

one beast,
arms raised to
surrender

or grasp,
torch-arms, arms
for flinging stone,

arms
frightened, furious
and proud—

and from
behind
the walls

we hear
their names for us
called out—

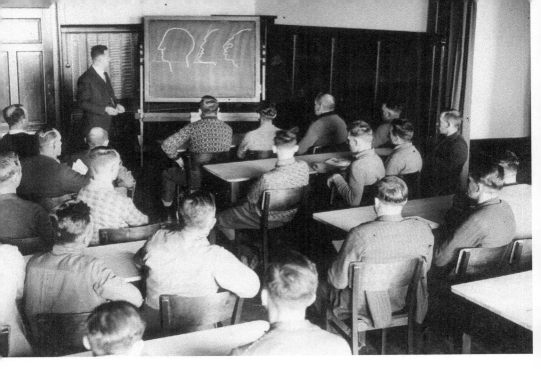

# Physiognomy 101

STEVEN SHER

**First they try to silence me**. They used to be respectful because the discourse was revered. But the attentive students of old are no more than ghosts haunting lecture halls. After forty years in academe, I am something of an anachronism myself. Noticeably old and white. Monogamous—still love my wife. Outwardly religious and not politically correct. I am different from anyone they know. I am all the things my students aren't. My directness violates their "safe space." I provoke them merely by my presence. When one coed sees that I am her professor, she flees from the class the very first day and never returns, claiming she can't be in the same room with one of them. She believes we are evil, my people have "horns." Everything I believe and teach contradicts the illusions they have been spoon fed from the womb. When one of my remarks undermines these views, they threaten they will get me fired and banned from social media. I retreat behind my desk, reluctant to challenge them. They intently study every mannerism; how I talk, wrestling air, with my

---

**About the Photo:** Adult class in racial theory, Gransee Germany, September 1933.

hands. They fixate on my differences: my head covering and dark beard, my pronounced nose and droopy eyelids, my high sloping forehead, fleshy lips and hairy hands. When I chance to walk between the rows among them, I call on someone inattentive in the back. He calls me a bigot for picking on him. I want to scream at his illogic but recognize the danger that I face. Other students, ready to record my response and any impending physical confront-ation, busy themselves sending texts and tweets from their seats right under my nose. A few are talking on their cell phones loud enough for all to hear. Headphones on, the rest are lost in their laptops. I recognize the plot to marginalize my authority. When the class ends and they storm for the door, I collect the papers they have left behind, doodlings meant to be found: *the professor*! with a long hook nose, narrow beady eyes and scraggly beard; completed games of Hangman with the stick figures bearing my name; a bull's eye on a rendering of my back—sometimes my wife finds spitballs stuck to the back of my jacket when I come home; crude ethnic jokes and swastikas.

**Then they try to scare my family.** Someone spray paints swastikas on the side of our house, hurls rotten eggs against the front windows and the door. I find threatening notes under the welcome mat or clamped beneath the windshield wipers of our car. News clippings purporting how terrible my people are and the resulting global condemnation are stuffed in the mailbox. Dolls' heads are impaled on the fence around our yard. The most visible of our coreligionists receive a Hitler birthday card in the mail. It threatens to cleanse the community of its degenerative elements. When I venture out, I see our faces on wanted posters about town like in the gunslinging Old West. We are this generation's desperadoes, wanted dead or alive. The profiling is constant. Unmarked cars follow me around town. My wife is afraid to go anywhere alone. Our children aren't spared, pariahs in the playground, taunted by their peers. In our daughter's kindergarten class, the walls are lined with images that give her nightmares: gaunt faces peering through a barbed wire fence; young men hurling rocks, their faces, save for the eyes, masked by scarves as smoke and fire rise about them; a mob applauding rockets being launched at innocents; a blackened shell of a school bus burning. In assembly, marching on stage, her classmates chant, "They hide behind every rock and tree," raising plastic guns in victory into the air. She plays one of the prisoners, hands bound and standing in a row with other sad-looking children.

**Then they come for our people**. An accuser stands each day out in the quad recruiting students with grand gestures and with charm, a bullhorn exhorting another "big lie," engaging faculty who soon embrace him, planting the seeds of solidarity, filling their heads with horrors done to those he loves. Concurrently, the old canards, stereotypic cartoons and blood libels appear in the student paper, circulate on lampposts and in stairwells, behind glass notice boards beside official bulletins. The administration is unsympathetic. When we bring speakers to campus, their messages are mocked and they are shouted down, the guards extricating them from the belligerent crowd while our accuser simply sits with folded arms among the students in the back, nodding as the chants grow bolder, grinning as the fists thrust higher in the air. These visits are irrevocably cancelled. Now our students and faculty are desperate to blend in, hide their identities altogether, though anyone who looks the part is fair game. Few and isolated, we are called fascists to our face—*Worse than Nazis*—by the growing number of accusers. Agents of hate and mayhem, they spit at us on the street. Our offices offer no sanctuary. When we arrive, we find garbage piled outside the door, a puddle of urine, its stench permeating the corridor, stuffed animals hung in effigy. We are greeted by crude caricatures and curses on the chalkboards in our classrooms. There are resolutions afoot to sack faculty and limit admissions, ban religious head coverings and beards. Our practices are provocations. *Where is Hitler when you need him?* Someone with a bullhorn prods their chanting in the quad. One shoves a crude sign in my face. A sheriff's deputy steps between us. Tightening my resolve, I pass this pack of barking dogs. A small hard object bounces like a bee off my chin. I quicken my step and wrap my arms like crossed swords over my head. A roar goes up behind me, a slap of reality across the cheek of flickering courage. "Blood for blood," someone shouts. "Towels. Hurry," someone counters. A colleague is led into the building drenched with blood. She is hysterical, flailing arms beyond calming, when someone throws several towels over her head and begins to wipe her briskly as if she were on fire. The brave few who stand up to this bullying are routed. A fist flies in a coed's face, breaking her glasses, sending her to the ground like a shattered figurine. Their nerve deserts them and they scatter, their hunters in hot pursuit. Rocks crash through glass. Broken signs and flyers litter the lawn, an omen of fresh corpses.

**Lastly they contend with G-d**. This accuser stands behind a lectern. There are no big-nosed, low-browed faces drawn on the board behind him, no claims made under the guise of "science." Rather, a map of the world is posted in front of the room, our homeland expunged. He disputes our history, picks apart our holy texts, dismisses our beliefs. He claims that he opposes hate. His students are alert and locked on every word; nothing can break their connection. He says we are a malignancy, hated among the nations, that must be isolated and destroyed. "G-d won't defend them. He doesn't hear their prayers. He's abandoned them." The accuser steps out from behind his lectern in full view, shaking his hand, one extended finger pointing at the ceiling. He demands to be shown G-d's glory at once—it is his right—to be placed in the cleft of the rock where Moses stood and saw the back of G-d in passing—no one can see G-d's face and live. He expects to see that G-d looks nothing like my people. He is stunned to learn with his last breath that G-d has seen it all.

# Dog Walter and the Walther Pistol

MARK BUDMAN

Hallo, my name is Kurt Müller. I'm the third boy in the first row in this photograph, marching on the cobblestones. A few steps away from *Herr* Von Schirach and *Herr* Streicher. I'm Aryan. I'm blond. I'm 12. I love flags and crowds and military music. Everyone looks at me and thinks: this boy is a real German soldier. An *Übermensch*.

My dog is Walter, a Doberman pinscher. I teach him tricks. He bit me only once, and I hit him with a stick. Now, he knows who the boss is. He's a keen dog.

I just lied to you. I don't really have a dog. We have no room for him in our cave, and nothing to feed him. But I imagine he's there. I love him. He bites Brüno when the guy is mean to me.

---

**About the Photo:** Baldur von Schirach (saluting), leader of the Hitler Youth, and Julius Streicher (in light-colored jacket), editor of the anti-Semitic newspaper, "Der Stuermer," review a parade of Hitler Youth in Nuremberg. 1933.

My friend is Fritz, he marches behind me. I'm taller by a head, and I can kick him in the pants. I love marching, I hate Jews and communists, and I wear a cool uniform: military boots, grey knee socks, shorts, and brown tunic. I got it when I turned 10. Why can't they make the sock brown? Good thing they are not wool. Wool is scratchy.

I just lied to you. Fritz is not my friend. He's rich, and he stays away from guys like me. They have their own gang.

I live in a two-room cave in Nuremberg with my *Mutti*, my veteran Papa with a missing leg, my married sister Anna, her scoundrel husband Brüno, her screaming baby, and my whore sister. Brüno works for a butcher. He makes little money, and he drinks *Schnaps*, and he stinks. All the meat he steals from work, he eats by himself. My whore sister makes more than him. If not for her, we would starve. She cries at night when she thinks everyone's asleep.

I just lied to you. My real name is Gereon, but I call myself Kurt, and I want everyone to call me that. Gereon is too church-y.

I know my Papa doesn't sleep much, but when he does, he shouts in his dream. Gas! *Panzer*! Shelling! At war, he made it all the way to *Gefreiter* before he was wounded. It's a big deal.

I just lied to you. *Gefreiter* isn't much of a rank. It's just one step above the private. Wait. Wasn't the *Führer* also a *Gefreiter*?

My *Mutti* doesn't want me to be in the *Hitlerjugend*. She wants me to sing in a church. She says I have angelic voice. I hate churches. They smell too sweet, like someone just died there. They say don't kill, but we, Germans, must kill. We don't have enough space.

A communist family lives in the flat below. I drop a frying pan on the tiled kitchen floor when I get up to drink some water at night. Brüno kicks me in the pants because I wake him. But it's worth it if I can wake up the communist family.

Jews don't live in our building. They are rich. Even richer than Fritz. They live in good flats with bathtubs, plenty of heat in the winter, and electric fans in the summer. I don't see them often, but their noses are bent like the number 6. We call it the Jewish Six. They have horns under their hats, black hair all over, and they stink. Not like Bruno. Bruno is an Aryan. *Herr* Streicher's *Der Stürmer* says they stink like sulfur. I don't know what sulfur is, but it must smell bad. I haven't seen any Jews, but *Der Stürmer* and our teachers tell us about them. They tell us Jews and Communists are the same, but Jews are worse. Communists are still German inside.

One day, we will go to tear up Jewish stores. I don't know which stores are Jewish, but they will tell me.

I hope, one day, we'll break a pet store, and I'll get myself a puppy. It's OK. The puppies are not Jewish. The puppies are Aryan. I'll call him Walter. I'll say, heel, Walter, heel, and everyone will be afraid of me. I'll grow up to be a *Sturmbannführer*. When I'll give an order, everyone will say *jawohl* and do it.

I will get a Walther pistol. Dog Walter and the Walther pistol. Got it? I will kick Fritz and Brüno in their pants. I will kill some Jews and communists. Two Jews for every one Communist. Everyone will be afraid of me, and I will be rich. I will kick some Jews out, and get their rich flat. I will give my family enough money for my sister to stop whoring. Until then, I will march on cobblestones and dream.

# Books Fly like Birds

ROBERT PERRY IVEY

History has a mean habit of writing itself
just after it has been unwritten. What burns here
is lost, but never forgotten and Berlin is not Alexandria.
I wonder if the crowds,
their faces painted with man's most deadly sins, pride and apathy,
realize that books are a country's cultural currency.
If a country bans books, then it is broke.
If a country burns books, then it is broken,
and its shadow covers whole maps
in ash-grey as a Nazi's uniform—

**About the Photo:** A member of the SA throws confiscated books into the bonfire during the public burning of "un-German" books on the Opernplatz in Berlin, May 10, 1933; Still from a motion picture.

one arm extended, tossing books upon the pyre.
The next step: kids in cages, families in cattle cars
with their fingers hanging through fence squares.
But here, in town square, there is a show
that flushes faces with the hues of fire.
Soldiers, priests, bakers and boys
turn their backs to it for what seems to be
ages. And when they finally look,
the spines crackle and split; the binding, the covers' skin
bleeds, melts, and runs;
ink, poems, lines lovelier than life,
art, craft, profound truths, lazy lies,
the beautiful record and terrible facts of being human
roar deafening rage and ear-splitting squeal before they ascend
warm and lush from leaf after leaf after leaf of paper.

The steps to domination are no mystery:
every empire (Sumerian, Egyptian, Roman,
German, English, and American) has laid it out plainly:
divide and conquer brother against brother,
children against parents, red vs blue; destroy maps—
rewrite your own; disintegrate museums, schools,
language, art and letters and facts—
replace with your own, no matter how obvious the untruth.

But, remember this: books flare and fly like birds
when phrases are burned, linger on pale ash
as words glow golden on embers, smoke wisps
and whispers on the wind. The faces on those book covers,
the truths and poetry of words, rise up.

# The Other

PETER SERCHUK

We're not very good after all.
Perhaps we were only the cast or rind,
the nails and shards left behind when
whichever God shaped the sand and sky
perfected his man with a soul elsewhere.

So there's not much news in looking back
to '33: The arson of evil ignited, its blaze
conceded or ignored, Germany soon ready
to settle scores: Europe too weak to blink and
America too weary to care what was happening over there.

**About the Photo:** U.S. demonstration against Nazi treatment of German Jews; those leading the demonstration included Rabbi Stephen S. Wise (hat in hand), New York, 1933; a book burning in Germany occurred on the very same day.

Every despot climbs his ladder by making demons
of some other. For Hitler, Jews were an easy mark
with their shops, their hats and shuls.
Those who waited for a parting sea knew
their bible but forgot their history.

And evil often comes with genius. By '33
Nazis had already woven themselves into the stars
& stripes: In the Congress, the State Department,
Mr. Hoover's FBI. Little wonder reports of atrocities
disappeared or fell on earless heads.

Still, Dr. Deutsch and Rabbi Wise persevered;
Lead a march, a hundred thousand strong all the way
to Battery Park. Which made every Jew feel safer—
who lived inside New York. The rest of America
ate their peas and left their dishes in the sink.

From there the story wails like an old, familiar tune.
Eight long years of invasion, genocide, annihilation;
While back home sunny skies feigned blindness to
the black moon… Goebbels and Lindbergh scrubbing
the air: Patriotic Americans have nothing to fear.

And so all was left to conscience, humanity's great orphan.
It would take the kamikazes to give the nation open eyes.
Not for Jews or Poles, Chinese or Dutch or the millions
more who died. But for fear they themselves might be
the other, once Hitler landed stateside.

# Flying African

GEOFFREY PHILP

Jesse, I can hardly imagine the weight
on your shoulders as you filed through the stadium,
flags flapping in the wind, nervous soldiers
marching behind to protect you from crowds
of young girls screaming, "Wo ist Jesse?"
while up in the stands the Fuhrer received
adulation from his adoring audience,
then sat and joked with his captains
about the superior genes of their athletes,
crouched in the shadow of a fence
where starved faces would peer
through barbed wire. But on that day you
exposed the lie that had stalked

**About the Photo:** American Olympic runner Jesse Owens and other Olympic athletes compete in the twelfth heat of the first trial of the 100m dash at the 1936 Olympics held in Berlin.[1]

you through segregated hotels and rest rooms
with signs that read, "Whites Only,"
and ran as if you were striding the air
away from their hate, like your father did
when he left the South, away from flaming
crosses and hooded Klansmen, following
his dream of freedom, like in the story
of our ancestors, which was passed from mouth
to hand in barbershops, soup kitchens, stoops
in Harlem, about the flying Africans
tired of scars, whips, chains, the Massa's
thunder, who stomped their feet, raised
their hands above their heads and sang,
"Today we are going home to Mount Zion!"

## Note

1    Owens won the race. He ultimately took first place in the event, finishing the race in 10.2
seconds, a record time; however, the record was disallowed by German officials, who claimed
that Owens had had the benefit of a tailwind. August 3,1936. Hitler saw the Games as an
opportunity to promote his government and ideals of racial supremacy and anti-Semitism and
the official Nazi party paper, the Volkischer Beobachter wrote in the strongest terms that Jews
should not be allowed to participate in the Games. When threatened with a boycott of the
Games by other nations, Hitler appeared to allow athletes of other ethnicities from other
countries to participate. However, German Jewish athletes were barred or prevented from
taking part by a variety of methods and Jewish athletes from other countries (notably the US)
seem to have been side-lined in order not to offend the Nazi regime.

# Bystander

NANCY NAOMI CARLSON

It takes two to bully, maybe three:
Bully, scapegoat, the one who looks away.
Words, like fire, heat up by degrees.

A fire starves without fuel, air and heat
And someone to turn their back on the flames.
It takes two to bully, maybe three

Or an army rifling through pockets and sleeves,
And someone to shoot the scene in black and gray.
Words, like bullets, heat up. By degrees,

Unions are banned, protesters bleed,
Marx is burned, fissures form in glass panes.
It takes two to bully, maybe three

**About the Photo:** Police search in Berlin with SA standing by, 1933.

When the housefrau sees only the dust she sweeps
Or the shopkeeper pulls down the blinds at mid-day.
Words, like mobs, heat up by degrees

Even in countries where twitter feeds
wildfires of hate.
It takes two to bully, maybe three.
Words, like ovens, heat up by degrees.

(THE POEM IN GERMAN)

# Zuschauer

Zum Schikanieren braucht man zwei, vielleicht auch drei:
Rüpel, Sündenbock, derjenige, der den Blick abwendet
Worte, wie Feuer, setzen allmählich die Hitze frei.

Ein Feuer verhungert ohne Brennstoff, Luft und Einheizerei
Und jemanden, der sich von den Flammen abwendet.
Zum Schikanieren braucht man zwei, vielleicht auch drei

Oder eine Armee, die Taschen und Ärmel durchwühlt, wie Plünderei,
Und jemanden, der die Szene in schwarz und grau ablichtet.
Worte, wie Patronen, erhitzen sich. Schritt für Schritt dabei,

Werden Verbände verbannt, bluten Protestler nach der Reihe,
Wird Marx verbrannt, sind die Glasscheiben als zerklüftete Scherben geendet.
Zum Schikanieren braucht man zwei, vielleicht auch drei

Wenn beim Kehren alles außer Staub für die Hausfrau ist einerlei
Oder wenn schon mitten am Tag der Ladenbesitzer Fensterläden schließend den Tag beendet.
Worte, wie der Mob, setzen allmählich die Hitze frei

Sogar in Ländern wo Twitter, immer dabei,
Wildfeuer des Hasses füttert und entsendet.
Zum Schikanieren braucht man zwei, vielleicht auch drei.
Worte, wie Öfen, setzen allmählich die Hitze frei.

(GERMAN TRANSLATION BY EVA LIPTON-ORMAND)

# Midnight Cake

ALEJANDRO ESCUDE

> *Every living creature that swarms will be able to live*
> *wherever this stream goes; the fish will be very*
> *abundant once these waters have reached there.*
> *It will be wholesome, and everything will live*
> *wherever this stream goes.*
>
> —Ezekiel 47:9

It could be any bureaucratic sun;
the orbiting planets, offices. There is a hatted woman
turned, an older man turned—some are smiling
as if sanity were in the breadcrumbs for the pigeons.
A balding man leans into a document, his face

**About the Photo:** German Jews at Palestine Emigration Office, 1935. After World War I the name Palestine Offices was applied to Zionist "consulates" in the Diaspora countries charged with the organization, regulation, and implementation of Jewish immigration to Palestine.[1]

too close to the sheet, the pen too close to his chin.
Is he doodling a fly into the paper? Does he know
the fly is a child suffocating in the arms of his grandfather?
From afar, the photograph could be a clump of scattered leaves.
The faces like pale bark. No spaces between the bodies.
Even the building is circumspect. That is what a dictator does
to the gravity of meaning: black, white, black, white;
how history comes to us in photographs. As if they were,
"simpler times." But everything has always been takeover.
Booming, militant voices. Everywhere, the promise of patriotism
and the slow, aching candles of religion. Is the ceiling light on
in the corner of the photo? That Guernica lamp?
That tie and that tie and that tie. Coffin-bodies, David's stars
pinned to thin chests. Oh how the dust is always silent!
Especially in the hollowed places. "Wake up!"
We wish to shout. "Put down the paperwork and run!"
There is a radio on God's bedside, streaming Goodman's
"Darn That Dream." The clarinet transforms itself
from instrument to machine gun and back again.
You have found yourself mute and madly in love.
Suddenly a horse, a horse-drawn carriage, an infant eaten
by the clamping bomb-jaws of a booted giant.
Couldn't the radio have taught you about the species of lies?
Couldn't the radio have swallowed the swastika flies?
No, you were on your own. Ladies and gentlemen,
I present to you the anti-Semitic brute, and his orchestra,
the racist nincompoops, straight from the netted heart of hell.
Do you hear its beat? Can you hear it, clear as a bell?
There are Fridays flopping like dying fish in the drawers
of the Palestinian Emigration Office. Government fishes
each in their own plot. The truth like a slice of midnight cake
to choke the strange, ambitious corporal who strides
toward a nuclear family like a hound and forces each one down
to the frozen ground, to be searched again and again.

## Note

1    In the 1920s and 1930s the Palestine Office distributed the immigration "certificates" issued by
     the Mandatory government to the Jewish Agency. Zionism began at the end of the 19th century
     in Eastern Europe, pursuing the return of the Jewish people to their ancestral home. Although
     other territorial solutions were considered, a state in Palestine came to be seen as the foremost
     goal for the movement.

# *Kinder* Gardens

SU HWANG

> *Give me your tired, your poor, your huddled masses*
> *yearning to breathe free.*
>
> —Emma Lazarus, The New Colossus

Rhododendrons bud from seed: too many shooting
stars—they grow up so fast to die, extinguished

in a blink—or wince. We forget celestial bodies
exist—(oh starry night, twinkle twinkle little star,

---

**About the Photo:** Jewish refugee children wave at the Statue of Liberty as the SS President Harding
steams into New York harbor, June 3, 1939.[1]

star of David in a bell jar)—long before & after
chronicled human folly: making our children weep.

Over & over, why we insist on infliction—this animal
drive from crusades to battlefields to darkened

chambers—we refuse to tend our gardens. Isn't the
moon balm enough for us to master the art of

magical thinking? Abundant when we, too, were
children. No need to subtract or expunge liberties;

bounty on this rock is plenty especially when we're
free to bloom—yet we let history repeat, incapable

of capturing the wonder that used to come so easily.
I'll only know motherhood in the ways we keep

things alive—even if it's just a matter of the mind.
No need to give up a pound to grasp we reap what

we do *not* sow. Maybe this is why I keep plastic
plants, for neglect yields anemic harvests. But still—

I want to surround every outline of life, trace the edges
with my eyes & fill them with wonder as if we are

forever children—not monsters spreading doom.

## Note

1   These children are among a group of fifty Jewish refugees (25 boys and 25 girls) from Vienna,
    aged 5 to 14, who are en route to Philadelphia, where they will be placed with foster families.
    The children were accompanied by Gilbert J. Kraus, a Philadelphia attorney, and his wife
    Eleanor, who had worked for months to secure their admission into the U.S.

# Night of the Broken Glass

PHILIP TERMAN

Glass lasts a million years.
Where are these remnants?

If they could speak, would they voice
The history of their shattering?

Was the glass sorted and washed
And crushed and melted

And molded into bottles?
These slivers, where do they reside?

---

**About the Photo:** Germans pass by the broken shop window of a Jewish-owned business that was destroyed during Kristallnacht. November 10, 1938.[1]

Can each shard represent
A fragment, sharp and fragile,

Of a scattered soul? Isn't
A soul similar to glass, hard

And brittle, transparent or
Translucent, vulnerable,

Easily cracked, as they are here,
Burst like razored shrapnel,

Thursday, November 10, 1938,
On this storefront sidewalk?

Pedestrians, overcoated, marching,
as if on command, on their way to work,

Gripping briefcases, pause,
Glance briefly at the jagged map

of emptiness that only a few hours ago
was the window display blocks of granite,

for repairing roads, were heaved through
to shape into a new country of hatred.

A window can be a mirror.
When, in the dead of night,

As the citizens approached
Lichtenstein Taschen and Co.,

Did they recognize, in the reflection,
Their own shadowed and contorted shapes?

And thus the destruction began.

## Note

1   Kristallnacht ("Crystal Night") also referred to as the Night of Broken Glass, was a pogrom
    against Jews throughout Nazi Germany on 9–10 November 1938, carried out by SA
    paramilitary forces and German civilians. The German authorities looked on without
    intervening. The name Kristallnacht comes from the shards of broken glass that littered the
    streets after the windows of Jewish-owned stores, buildings, and synagogues were smashed.

## Body Boarding

GRETCHEN PRIMACK

I used to have a name. I had hands: Someone pinned the hat.
I had a mouth: Someone smiled and savored when food

was about savor, a cup of frothed chocolate,
a brothed soft carrot coin. I had a heart:

someone's chest hummed like a cello's chest
when the feelings packed in like music, like urges.

Someone believed she was packed with heat
and would die without it.

Now I am cold and shelled and a survivor,
nothing but. Now this is a body boarding

---

**About the Photo:** The Joseph Family boarding the St. Louis, 1939. MS St. Louis was a German
ocean liner.[1]

and taking space. Making its way not home.
They don't understand how warm and mine

my blood was. What moves through me dissolved
its thumbprints until I became nothing but a form

bound for somewhere not home: Cuba.
On that island a child by the dock will see this thin

grim line where a grin spent years and know
as much about me as I do now.

## Note

1    In 1939 the MS St. Louis set off on a voyage in which her captain, Gustav Schröder, tried to find
     homes for over 900 Jewish refugees from Germany. Due to countries' immigration policies
     based on domestic political realities, rather than humanitarian grounds, they were denied entry
     to Cuba, the United States, and Canada. The refugees were finally accepted in various
     European countries, including Belgium, the Netherlands, the UK, and France. It is estimated
     that approximately a quarter of them died in death camps.

# The Day Before

SUE WILLIAM SILVERMAN

Dawn pins the night's monstrous
constellations on you. Day after day
fingers numb from sewing. If only

you could stitch your soul
to something to forestall the theft of
your history, your heart. You.

Only a few brutal hours remain.
Unstoppable hands *tick, tick, tick*
the day forward. The confiscation

**About the Photo:** In November of 1939, subsequent to the German invasion, Jews in Poland were required to wear the Jewish Badge (Star of David). Jewish women wearing yellow Jude stars are walking in the street, near a park. This photo was taken before the establishment of the Lodz ghetto. the assumed location,1939–1940.

of abstractions: *joy, love, future.*
What happens to cousins, candles,
first kisses, final good-byes?

Remnants of ginger cake, weak tea.
Formless dresses, blown ghostly,
abandoned on clotheslines.

The wind-scatter of rouge,
ribbons, bits of lace, white doilies
through blank open windows.

The loss of hair once hid
beneath your checkered raincoat.
You can only be someone

they would not have you be.
Who will stop it? No one.
The tyranny of *tick, tick, tick.*

Today you see everything
and nothing; fear nothing
and everything. Only

unanswerable questions remain:
where will the throb of your heart
go when it stops? Where will veins go

when blood foams under your tongue?
Where will the flutter of lungs go
when slowed to a shudder?

Breath slips past lips. Spirit fades.
Yellow stars flame across night
only to be extinguished in the Baltic.

Desperation is combustible.
You are a narrative fragment
lost in the smoke of history.

What trace survives?
You are the last fragile
light before the black.

# PART I ESSAY: An historical and geopolitical perspective

## Interwar Europe and the Scourge of 'Identity Politics'

PAUL VINCENT

Explanations for the course and outcome of European politics during the interwar years (1918–1939) are varied and complex. Many are resolutely attached to the terms of the Versailles Treaty. Although one of several documents fashioned to conclude the First World War at the Paris Peace Conference and ensure a lengthy peace, many contemporaries—not only Germans—perceived Versailles as unnecessarily harsh.[1] It was soon stamped "a Carthaginian peace;" thereby likening its terms to Rome's brutal response over 2000 years earlier to Carthage after the three Punic Wars: the Romans utterly destroyed the ancient city, sold its citizens into slavery, and plowed salt into the ruins to ensure that nothing again could be grown. While common sense and analysis have long diminished the importance of Versailles among historians, one cannot remove the *perception* that the Germans had been egregiously treated following World War I. It encouraged Britain's appeasement of a "maligned" Germany and America's resolve to forswear European political crises. There are, nonetheless, two interrelated factors which, while crucial to understanding Europe's geopolitics, are often overlooked. The first is that Germany and Russia, those states with the greatest potential power, had been enormously weakened by World War I and might be seen as "belly up" in 1919. It was inconceivable that they'd remain so. Both would reject democracy and the status quo while by the 1930s embracing totalitarianism—one focused on racial ideology, the other on an ideology aimed at fashioning a classless society. Not discounting the importance of Versailles or America's pivot in the 1920's and 30s to a posture of political isolation; these factors must be viewed as more urgent, especially in a Europe now absent a balance of power. They are an important piece of the framework for what follows.

Writing in the 1970s, George F. Kennan revealed that he had come to see the First World War as "the great seminal catastrophe of [the twentieth] century."[2] That it took Kennan more than fifty years to draw this conclusion—or, at least, to publish it—is significant. World War I took the lives of more than ten million soldiers and roughly an equivalent number of civilians (3.7 million for the

Allied Powers, 6.8 million for the Central Powers). For contemporaries, these numbers were unprecedented—catastrophic, to echo Kennan. Yet, the Spanish influenza pandemic of 1918-19 killed at least 50 million people.[3] While *at a minimum* this number equals the casualty estimates from the war, Kennan makes no mention of Spanish flu, let alone tag it a seminal catastrophe. Distinction rests in the fact that the mortality generated by the war was human induced, a result of violent and premeditated bloodletting. Moreover, that experience evolved into something later labeled "total war"; as the term implies, war was to be waged not simply against the enemy's men in uniform but against the state itself, including its assets and civilian population. In the case of the Ottoman Empire, the targeted civilians were sometimes located within the country's own borders—i.e., the Turks genocidal treatment in 1915 of the local Armenian population, an episode that proved a harbinger. The First World War informed widespread populations that ordinary men had the capacity to kill indiscriminately in vast numbers, with survivors thereafter returning home to work in mines and factories, run businesses, milk cows, teach students, and raise families. It exposed a reality both bewildering and frightful. For some it dovetails neatly—too neatly—with the thesis that the war brutalized postwar politics, a proposition compelling especially to students of Germany and Italy (or Soviet Russia), but less so when one's focus is Britain and France, where postwar violence was not appreciably greater than it had been before 1914.

Yet, Kennan's "seminal catastrophe" should be viewed as something more than a window on humanity's capacity for mass violence. By and large, the war set in motion in 1914 was a struggle between multi-ethnic empires: the German Empire, the Austro-Hungarian Empire, the Russian Empire, the Ottoman Empire. As the calamity unfolded, far exceeding anything most could have imagined, its character metastasized. Gradually, class and ethnic antagonisms subverted loyalty to those multi-ethnic empires so that, by 1917, the violence of war was increasingly politicized. While not universal, the transformation— Robert Gerwarth calls it "a tectonic shift"—explains both the Bolshevik Revolution and the disintegration of Russia's vast empire.[4] The Russian experience served as prelude to the collapse of the multi-ethnic empires that had euphorically joined the war in 1914-15. Moreover, the Bolshevik Revolution and the political maxim of Moscow's new regime aroused a counterrevolutionary ethos not just within the borders of the former Russian Empire but stretching through much of the European continent. The varied ethnicities within the now collapsed empires had not failed to recognize their differences before 1914; however, their prewar vision of expanded autonomy within multi-ethnic empires only rarely evolved into a demand for national independence. The war had forged unintended consequences.

In a well-worn legend, a peasant claims that he was born in Russia, married in Poland, raised a family in the Soviet Union, and was preparing to die in Ukraine. He lived throughout his several decades in the same peasant hut, never abandoning the home of his parents and grandparents. Such was the twentieth-century experience of many living in East-Central Europe. Among the tragedies attached to Woodrow Wilson was his conviction that suppressed self-determination had triggered the Great War.[5] Addressing this grievance, he asserted, would make it "the war to end all wars." Looking back, were we to identify one factor that made life in interwar Central and Eastern Europe uncommonly precarious, if not always violent, it was the rise of the nation-state, the logical consequence of self-determination. A modern political invention, rooted in the eighteenth century, nationalism espoused the utopian and dangerous goal of homogeneous ethnicity.[6] Where either supposed or actual nation-states believed themselves separated by unjust borders from ethnic communities imagined to belong to them—or, vice versa, comprising remnants of ethnic groups that supposedly held no place in the new state—seething resentment was apt to turn violent, whether to defend vulnerable members beyond a new state's borders or to remove those deemed alien to the national community within these borders. To take an example, the resurrected state of Poland certainly comprised Poles (roughly two-thirds of a population of just over 27 million according to a 1921 census); however, a third of its inhabitants were Ukrainians, Byelorussians, Germans, Lithuanians, and, of course, Jews. If the Poles aimed to fashion an actual nation-state, the disposition of 9 million of its inhabitants posed a grievous problem. Similar preoccupations tormented Byelorussia, Ukraine, Germany, Austria, Czecho-slovakia, Hungary, Romania, Italy, the three Baltic States, and the hodge-podge entity of Yugoslavia, known in 1920 as the Kingdom of Serbs, Croats, and Slovenes.[7] Product of the Paris Conference, the League of Nations proved ineffectual in dealing with such problems.

The dream of realizing ethnically homogenous polities—i.e., the aspiration for a "real" nation-state—was a deadly interwar example of identity politics that might be judged the overriding geopolitical reality of interwar Europe from the Balkans to the Baltic States. Wherever the dream was either threatened or unsatisfied, a potential for violence existed. Set against the further reality of worldwide depression, it corrupted in particular the political landscape of small and insecure new states; not only did they threaten one another, they were in turn viewed as easy prey by the continent's larger powers. Ethnic violence even found outlet in Stalin's ruthless effort to attain a classless society.[8] When antipathy to "the Jew" focused the ethnic violence of virtually all of these states, it was often undergirded by the specious assertion that the Jew and Bolshevism were one and the same threat. Empty as it was, the claim had powerful roots. In the ferocious civil war that ripped Russian society, leading to as many as four million deaths, antisemitic pogroms were a common feature, especially in the western reaches of the former empire. Noting a comparatively large Jewish representation among the communist leadership, the anti-Bolshevik "White Russians" stigmatized the October Revolution as a Jewish conspiracy. Robert Gerwarth writes that the "anti-Judeo-Bolshevik card gave the Whites at least something popular with which to identify and it quickly led to outbreaks of anti-Semitic (sic) violence throughout the former Romanov Empire."[9] It was a conviction, moreover, that was not limited to the borders of that empire. Reinforcing a centuries-old narrative at the heart of traditional Christian anti-Judaism, that the Jews were responsible for the crucifixion of Jesus, it dovetailed neatly with that prewar fabrication, *The Protocols of the Elders of Zion*, claiming that the Jews conspired for world domination. So, while ethnic animosity served to divide German, Pole, and Ukrainian, all found considerable unity in their common hatred of the Jew.

Ethnic turmoil in Europe was largely mastered in the immediate aftermath of the Second World War, when widespread and often brutal ethnic cleansing transformed the 1919 dream of the nation-state into reality. But with the collapse of the Soviet bloc in the 1990s and the world refugee crisis of the early twenty-first century, a new version of ethnic violence resurfaced. In our contemporary world, it might be—indeed, it has been—labeled identity politics. When so-called "identity politics" is perceived to either privilege or disparage one group by comparison to others, the likelihood of violence should be taken as a given. Although the 21st-century world is vastly different from that of interwar Europe, the earlier period casts an ominous shadow.

## Notes

1   In addition to Versailles, the Paris Peace Conference produced the Trianon Treaty, ending the war with Hungary, the St. Germain Treaty, ending the war with Austria, the Neuilly Treaty, ending the war with Bulgaria, and the Sevres Treaty, supposedly ending the war with the Ottoman Empire.

2   George F. Kennan, The Decline of Bismarck's European Order (Princeton: Princeton University Press, 1979), p. 3. David Reynolds approaches the topic differently by entitling a recent book *The Long Shadow: The Legacies of the Great War in the Twentieth Century* (New York: Norton, 2013).

3    www.cdc.gov/flu/pandemic—resources/1918—pandemic—h1n1.html
4    It also helps account for the long-term collapse of the global empires of both Britain and France.
5    We must appreciate that the terms "Great War" and "World War" were used by people, our forebears, who could not imagine a second and worse such conflict, people who in the 1920s and most of the 1930s believed themselves living in an era labeled "postwar," not "interwar."
6    While nationalism may be of recent fabrication, tribalism dates back to man's origins. They hold much in common. To be fair and accurate, I'm writing here of exclusive nationalism, which demands ethnic uniformity; but there's also an inclusive nationalism, resting on common political beliefs, not on the fiction of common ancestry.
7    Although the Anatolian region of the new state of Turkey is not conceptually in Europe, it witnessed savage ethnic violence in the four years following the war. The resulting Treaty of Lausanne (1923) terminated Greek ambitions in Anatolia and led to the most brutal and comprehensive case of ethnic cleansing prior to the onset of the Second World War.
8    Stalin's destruction via purposeful starvation of the kulaks was conceived as the removal of a class enemy; however, it can also be viewed as an ethnic attack. Although numbers are still debated, with a minimum of 3 million and a maximum of 8 million starved to death, the numbers remain a powerful indicator of genocide carried out against Ukrainians and people living in the North Caucasus, where roughly 40 percent (one million) of the Kazakh population died in 1932–33.
9    Robert Gerwarth, *The Vanquished: Why the First World Failed to End*, (New York: Farrar Straus and Giroux, 2016), p. 89. When Gerwarth writes "the Whites" he's referencing an unsteady coalition of anti-communist forces variously known as the White Army, the White Guard, or simply the Whites. Founded in 1917 and comprised of Cossacks, nobles, peasants, and conscript volunteers, they numbered over three million and generated a civil war within the revolution. Their inability to coordinate their efforts led to their defeat and destruction by 1923.

## Recommended Further Reading

Berend, Ivan T. *Decades of Crisis: Central and Eastern Europe before World War II.* Berkeley: University of California Press, 1998.

Gerwarth, Robert. *The Vanquished: Why the First World War Failed to End.* New York: Farrar, Straus and Giroux, 2016.

Gerwarth, Robert, and John Horne, eds. *War in Peace: Paramilitary Violence in Europe after the Great War.* New York: Oxford University Press, 2012.

Hanebrink, Paul. *A Specter Haunting Europe: The Myth of Judeo-Bolshevism.* Cambridge: Harvard University Press, 2018.

Reynolds, David. *The Long Shadow: The Legacies of the Great War in the Twentieth Century.* New York: W. W. Norton, 2013.

Steiner, Zara. *The Lights that Failed: European International History, 1919–1933.* New York: Oxford University Press, 2005.

———. *The Triumph of the Dark: European International History, 1933–1939.* New York: Oxford University Press, 2011.

# PART II

# Forced Labor, Ghettos, Extermination

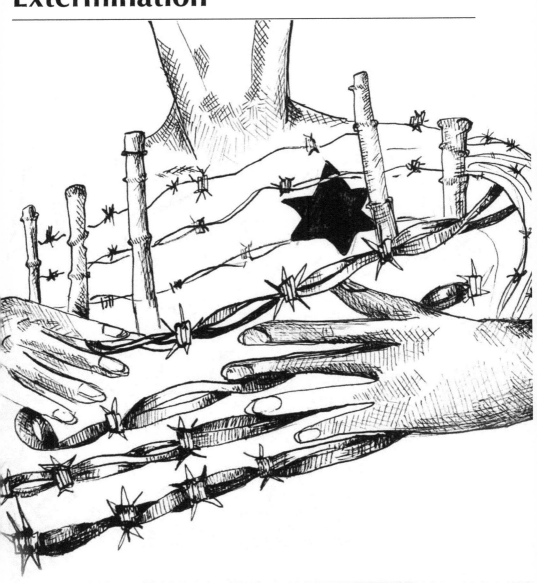

## Prelude to Part II

Forced Labor / Death Squads / Ghettos / The "Final Solution" / Concentration    Camps / Killing    Centers / Sympathizers / Perpetrators / Victims / Collaborators / Ordinary Citizens

# Viewfinder

BEN BANYARD

I saw them on the road near Konskowola that afternoon.
Without thinking I lifted my camera, closed one eye,
framed them and squeezed off the shot.

I thought they were simply a construction gang,
until later, when my neighbour explained

they were inmates forced to build their own prison,
work on the farms the Nazis seized.

Nowadays, with good behaviour, incarcerated men
might expect an early release.

---

**About the Photo:** Jewish men at forced labor carrying sections of barbed wire fencing along a road in Konskowola, Poland circa 1939–43.

They seemed almost cheerful; see how the one in the middle
almost smiles for the camera, the reflex impossible to resist.

In the darkroom, as the developer washed across the paper,
the truth came to me in waves.

The barbed wire snags my dreams all these years later,
as though their burden became mine in that shutter's blink.

## "A Vort Far A Vort"/Tit For Tat

### JUDITH BAUMEL

If they seem faceless — and they are in this
shot — anonymity was not unfolding in
the instant. Each possessed a face and each
possessed a name and each, within, some tales,
yes, bushels of tales, volumes of fables, each
one was a library of infinity.
Menakhem-Mendls, Sheyne Sheyndels, Motls.
They crowded at the Zasulye Yar,
faced east to the rope works and offered the camera's eye
their human selves with frank indifference,
defiance and disdain, worry and love.
The Nazi officer recording for

---

**About the Photo:** Over one thousand Jews including women and children from the Ukrainian town of Lubny, (Luben in Yiddish) ordered to assemble for resettlement, in an open field before they were massacred by Nazi Sonderkommando on the outskirts of the city on October 16, 1941.[1]

his propaganda unit saw with forced
neutrality the blur his subjects saw:
the brightness of that sunny morning. And
ironic fields. And the ravine. Over-
exposed. The earth unveiled a bitter charm.
Just weeks before, the same photographer
recorded Babi Yar filled to the brim,
the Sonderkommando cleaning up.
They mostly knew, these Jews who'd gathered near
their Kirov square and marched in columns here,
it wasn't *relocation*. Still, as things
became more clear, even the most tender
of them stripped as ordered, ran as ordered.
Please lend an ear, friend: once upon a time
a long, long time ago the citizens
of *Luben* were the Yiddish joke of their
Crown Rabbi just before his work required
the ironic pseudonym by which you know
him now, "Peace Unto You." The wild pogroms
changed him and so did marriage. *Luben* brought
him doubt. Such avaricious common folk.
Two angels walk beside us each *Shabbat*,
the other days it's our misfortune to
be human all alone in our distress.
The name our hero writer took was thus
a plea, a prayer, a possibility
to struggle with. A curse upon the town's
descendants who in 1941
would rasp *Shema, Shema,* not Sholem Aleichem.

## Note

1     Hebrew/Yiddish words used in the poem: the title "A Vort Far A Vort" is taken from Sholem
      Aleichem's story of the same title, literally translated as "a word for a word," in published
      translations of the story rendered as "Tit for Tat," Luben=Lubny, Shabbat=Sabbath,
      Shema=hear(lit.)refers to the central Jewish prayer "Shema Yisrael," "Hear O'Israel" an
      affirmation of Judaism and a declaration of faith in one God.

# In the Lodz Ghetto

## MARGE PIERCY

'Collaborator' was a dirty word
when I grew up along with quisling,
fink, snitch—one who betrayed,
joined the powers that control,
sold out to the enemy. But

in a deadly mess, more than
coerced, a misstep fatal, options
fewer than unicorns, how shall
we judge the Judenrat, elders
mostly, who ran the ghettoes

---

**About the Photo:** Jewish council chairman Mordechai Chaim Rumkowski signs a document at a wedding in the Lodz ghetto.[1]

to save German contact with
our dirty selves? Did they see
themselves as protectors? Did
they hope facilitating Nazi rule
would save them? [it didn't].

An ethical swamp. In the Lodz
Ghetto where Jews were jammed
into crowded flats, fed little,
worked much, the Judenrat tried
to make normal, marrying those

whose marriage would be sweet
perhaps but short. Resistance
made them nervous: we'll be
punished, shot, starved more.
Don't make trouble. Obey! Quiet!

Jews had so often survived
by acting meek, keeping eyes
lowered, it felt almost natural.
Did they make life a little better
or just ease the way to murder?

Pretending to normality, business
as sort of usual, does that work
in the long run, trying to appease?
What is the cost of going along
while the world they knew burns?

## Note

1    Called Judenraete (sg., Judenrat), these Jewish municipal administrations were required to
     ensure that Nazi orders and regulations were implemented. Jewish council members also
     sought to provide basic community services for ghettoized Jewish populations. Forced to
     implement Nazi policy, the Jewish councils remain a controversial and delicate subject. The
     members of the Jewish councils faced impossible moral dilemmas. Often forgotten in the
     debates over the culpability of the Jewish councils and the Jewish police are the efforts of many
     Jewish council members and officials in their employ to provide a variety of social, economic,
     and cultural services under the brutal and difficult conditions in the ghettos.

# Photograph of Jews Probably Arriving to the Lodz Ghetto Circa 1941–1942

ELLEN BASS

Why is a horse here
alongside the train? Two horses

yoked with leather harnesses, light
silvering their flanks

in the midst of the Jews
descending? Where is the driver

taking the cart, loaded
with wooden planks?

What is in the satchel
that weighs down the arm

---

**About the Photo:** Following the public announcement of the establishment of the Lodz (Poland) ghetto on February 8, 1940, Jews were expelled from all other parts of the city and moved into the ghetto area.[1]

of a woman in a dark coat,
her hair parted on the side?

A woman I could mistake
for my mother

in the family album. Only
my mother was in Philadelphia,

selling milk and eggs and penny candy
because her mother escaped the pogroms,

a small girl in steerage
crying for *her* mother.

What are the tight knots
of people saying to one another?

A star burns the right shoulder blade
of each man, each woman. Light strikes

each shorn neck
and caps each skull. No one is yet

stripped of all but a pail
or a tin to drink from and piss in.

Dread, like sun, sears the air
and breaks over the planes of their faces.

Light clatters down upon them
like stones, but we can't hear it.

Nor can we hear blood
thud under their ribs.

They will be led into the ghetto
and then will be led out to the camps,

but for now, the eternal now,
the light is silent,

silent the shadows
in the folds of their coats. The bones

of the horses are almost visible.
Their nostrils are deep, soft shadows.

And the woman
who could be but is not

my mother,
still carries her canvas bag

and, looking closer,
what might be a small purse.

## Note

1    164,000 Jews were imprisoned in the ghetto when it was sealed off on April 30, 1940. In 1941
     and 1942 an additional 38,500 Jews and 5,000 Roma (Gypsies) were resettled in the ghetto.

# Assassination

GREG HARRIS

Dicho Kanchev nudged open the door to the production trailer with his buttocks. His paunchy body in its gray suit followed, then his head with its flop of gray hair, his corrugated forehead, and finally his arms, which were tugging at an unseen girl, who giggled and said in German, "No, No, Dicho," and then, "You are so bad."

"And you are so good. I'm really your last hope against socialist sainthood."

She allowed herself to be pulled into the room. One of the East German stars. In the movie we were filming, she played a factory worker who is seduced by a manager and helps him—against her better judgment—divert shoes onto the black market. She is poisoned as part of the coverup, but her older sister unravels the scheme and gets the factory manager locked up for life. A happy ending!

---

**About the Photo:** Reichsfuehrer-SS Heinrich Himmler looks on as Reinhard Heydrich's casket is carried out from the Reich chancellery for burial. 1942[1]

"What makes you think I don't want socialist sainthood?" she said. She allowed him to keep tugging her as he sat down. "Hmm?" She was straddling him, and his answer was spoken into the valley of sweater between her breasts. That he would get her such roles! That in Bulgaria she would be a goddess...

That's when she looked up.

"Oh! Dicho, you said the trailer was empty. Hello, you're the accountant?"

Dicho didn't look at me. Who could blame him? He was rediscovering his youth. For some men, it's so well hidden, only fresh cleavage can reveal it.

"I don't—he didn't—oh I'm embarrassed," she said, then shrieked with laughter as his hand came up her side.

He wrapped his arms around her soothingly and said, still not looking at me, "It *is* empty. Natan was just leaving."

I gathered my papers—it wasn't a bad moment to collect signatures from the crew on recent expenditures—and left without saying a word.

I was the accountant. A decade ago I would have been in position to reprimand Dicho—was, I don't mean to brag, lead coordinator for film and media projects for the Ministry of Propaganda. If I hadn't entertained actresses in precisely Dicho's style, certainly I'd known, sipping wine across the table from some bright young thing—this East German girl, for instance, with her degree in mechanical engineering—that her eagerness to please had little to do with my own charm. So on the one hand, who was I to judge?

On the other—Dicho was shit on a shoe. The stink of his low cunning seemed to follow you from room to room.

Six months ago, when I was just starting as production accountant, I'd brought an irregularity in the film budget to his attention. Our project allotment had been exceeded by more than 10,000 leva, but I could document no source of the overruns. As I took the tram from this production trailer in Lozenets back to the Ministry of Propaganda to report it, I felt pride in my work—even, I'll admit, a fantasy of rapid promotion, and ultimately rehabilitation. If in just a few days' examination I could spot a discrepancy of this magnitude...how long would it be until I was restored to an office in the main building, perhaps to my old post!

Dicho's office in the Ministry of Propaganda was a bare white room too small for his body odor, with a desk that, had filmmakers ever seen it, would have haunted them as an abattoir of dreams. On one side, a stack of proposed scripts, with notes for proposed casting. On the other, scripts with Dicho's red grease pencil marks boxing in various pages and passages, and his typed notes explicating how this that or the other deviated from party interests and Marxist ideology. I used to receive such red-greased work on my desk, two floors above this, with a view over the Nevsky plaza that I now could not bear to think about.

The art of being lead coordinator had been to balance the artistic merits of a film against just how exhausting the effort would be to defend the greased-up passages to the censors above *me*.

Maybe Dicho sniffed my dislike as clearly as I sniffed the bacteria multiplying in his armpits. But I could tell, even before he took my ledger in hand, that this was going to go wrong. How wrong I didn't know; my every act, in those early days out of prison, felt like a shaking curtain that could be ripped back, and me thrown back into the interrogation rooms.

I averted my attention to the bookshelf, whose content seemed to correspond to the 1966 output of Narodna Koultoura's presses—the year, presumably, that he'd first felt the need to impress his superiors with his grasp of national culture. Some of the volumes came askew on one end where he must reach with some regularity for the rolls of toilet paper stashed behind.

"Well," he finally said. "I suppose you'll just have to find some way to cover it from the next film's budget. Don't let this happen again, whatever you do."

"But do you understand the cause? How can I prevent what I can't even document?"

He said, "Let's imagine you showed somebody these books, who was in a position to audit. What would they think?"

"Embezzlement."

"Precisely. Which is why I say, don't let this happen again. You can hardly afford even a shadow of suspicion, Natan. It was one of the reasons I *greatly hesitated* before taking you on board. So. Don't let this happen again." He closed the ledger decisively and handed it back to me.

And from then I knew what it would be like, working with Dicho. His crimes, my punishment. His embezzlements, my coverup. His actresses, my desk's damp patch.

My abject helplessness, my fantasies of garroting him with piano wire until his face ruptured. Doing to him what was done to me during five years' prison time, the dance with my torturer far more intimate than anything Dicho enjoyed with his starlets. They, after all, had limited use for each other. An afternoon. A few weeks, at most, until the next film was secured.

A re-educator needs access to your entire soul, to its last limits.

At end of day I dropped paperwork off at the office on Vasil Levski street. I tried to be in and out without speaking, but Grozdana Stainova called me over.

I had hired Grozdana, fresh from Sofia University's literature department, eight years ago. A providential move, it turned out, since she was the one who in pity took me back as an accountant. How she had changed, though. From a slim, dark girl with a ready smile, and unfeigned excitement about the works of our Bulgarian writers, she now had widened, her lips sagging at the corners like a toad's, the bones in her cheek buried under puffy flesh. Her eyes on me weary, guarded, lined. "There was a complaint," she said. "Dicho reported you were unnecessarily brusque to an actress; it cost her concentration. The scene will have to be reshot tomorrow."

This was Dicho's cunning. Having leveled this at me, he made it impossible for me to inform on him. "I didn't realize," I said.

"You can't afford to be a pimple, Natan. Don't be a pimple on anyone's ass."

"I won't," I said. "I have nothing but fond thoughts of Dicho and his actress."

"How in the world did you head up a department of propaganda, Natan, when you are this bad at lying?"

She allowed a crease to form at the corners of her mouth for a moment; it was a smile that I returned ruefully.

Sofia in the brave new winter of 1970 bears only passing resemblance to the city in which I grew up. Take my neighborhood. Concrete tower blocs, statues monotonous in their celebration of the revolutionary worker, locked doors, drawn shades. Barely even a café whose gleam and beckon might dispel the chill of the wind off Mount Vitosha. Even in the center of the city our squares, our boulevards, feel suppressed; a voice raised on the street is an invitation to be overheard. You scurry home to warm yourself, if you are lucky, with heat from a distant furnace, and *rakiya* from family in the provinces.

But I am a Jew; I have no family in the provinces. Or rather, the provinces are Jaffa and Netanya, across the Mediterranean, and for pity's sake let my family— who all moved to Israel after the war—never send me anything ever again.

Well, and I am not going to depend on pity. I have never told them my address, or that I am out of prison.

I breathe into my cupped palms to warm them before I can fumble my key into the lock. This is something I remember from the war, from the labor camps, how as the flesh thins around your bones, the cold reaches ever deeper. Twice now I have enjoyed the official hospitality of the Bulgarian state, first as a twenty year old yanked out of university and kept two years as slave labor, building railroads alongside my fellow sufferers. Second as a forty year old, a political prisoner, a suspected Israeli spy because of my brother's mailing me packages. One government fascist; one government socialist. Both agreed on having no use for Jews. And both seemingly agreed on winnowing me to 50 kilograms as if, in some mysterious accounting, they had determined this is as much flesh as ought to be allowed my Jewish skeleton.

What is it Shakespeare has harsh Shylock demand, in compensation for the indignities he suffers? A pound of flesh? The shock of that play, I remember from reading it, is the literalness of that demand. Bulgaria should be no less shocking, its requisition no less literal.

The key won't turn. Frowning, I turn it the other way, and hear the bolt slide home as it locks. For just a second I am dumbfounded. My instincts are that slow.

Then my heart bursts into painful jog, and I turn to flee down the corridor—to where, I don't know. I'm not thinking! Where does one hide from a state that will not let you leave, and takes away your last place to stay?

But the person inside is quicker. My door flies back. I turn in dread—and my daughter, Risa, is there.

My first thought, which I don't even try to excuse: she is with them. I am that convinced there is a 'them' inside, as there was a 'them' waiting for me that day, five years ago, when I came back to my office from lunch.

"Daddy?" she says.

She is the new Risa, the one I barely recognize. Serious of face, long of limb, awkwardly large of foot and hand, twelve years old and wearing one of her mother's blouses buttoned beneath her neck.

As for her recognizing me—that is a heartbreaking thought. What is left of the father I once was? Since my release we have spoken just once, in a formal session with my ex-wife. Your mother will know best how to raise you, I'd said; I will always adore you. She'd stared at me, the gaunt lines of my new face. She'd seemed—perhaps I am wrong—relieved to learn I would not be moving back in with her and her mother.

She does not know that I have hovered near her, on her walk to school. As a kind of disembodied protective spirit I've picked her up from the apartment, and dropped her off, aching to make myself known as she laughs with her friends—or more often treads, somber and alone. She goes to a new school now, the middle grades. The teachers do not know me.

"What are you—how—is your mother here, too?"

"She let me in, but she did not stay. Can you take me home, after?"

"After?"

While we talk we are choreographing an awkward dance, she backwards off her left foot, me forward as if eyes are pressed to peepholes all along the corridor—which they may well be. I try not to touch, not to be in range of each other where a hug becomes natural, and its avoidance obvious. She is formal, I am formal, and eventually I am in front of my hot plate and she standing just at the kitchen wall, one hand holding the other wrist like an anxious debutante.

"I have a school project," she says. "Mom said I should interview you, you would know more about it than anyone."

"What is it?" I ask. Dreading her answer. The punishment of state enemies?

Making oneself an unnecessary person? Graphomania? The notebooks I filled in prison are a pile half a meter deep in my closet. No one will ever read them but they are the most solid aspect of my being. My clothes dangle above them like sad wraiths. "And would you like some tea?"

"Thank you! Yes." For a moment, in relief, she sparks up and she's the girl I remember from five years ago, the quick-witted imp of six, who could not get enough of her father's stories.

I shake some leaves into the strainer and start the water boiling.

"It's about an assassination," she says. "During the war. Because it's for youth leadership my teacher wants us to come up with more than just the story. She said, 'Don't just recount the act of bravery as if you were cuckoos who can only repeat what you're told. Say something worthy of the heroism of the act."

I am astounded. This is language my daughter is now capable of speaking? This mocking irritation toward a teacher—this is something she can do, now? A rush of gratitude fills me, that life did not end when I thought it would, in the room in 5 Moskovska when they first took me in, when faced with my lack of anything to confess, and my unremorse, the interrogator found it necessary to draw such blood that his boot tracked it—tracked *me*—on the floor as he walked away.

Gratitude, too, that Maria my ex-wife had raised Risa to be this girl. This young woman in the making. That Maria had had the strength and wisdom to divorce me, to create space between us so that the state would not go after them, too.

Tears rose in my eyes; it was hard to hear for a moment, and I could see nothing. "Daddy?" Risa said again, the same tone as at the door. And I commanded myself to swallow everything. I did not want to alarm her.

"I'm sorry," I said. "There were so many assassinations. Your uncle Baruch—" But I did not want her to learn of her uncle Baruch, the one whose packages from Jaffa had condemned me. Let there be no traffic between us, even in stories. Even though Baruch had been the more active partisan in the war, had run socialist missions that involved assassinations of the fascist police chief in Vratsa and elsewhere.

Such heroism no longer mattered, now that he was on the other side of the Mediterranean.

"You, father, did you assassinate?" She asks as if it was like playing chess! The scale of her questions, her comprehension. I must not exceed them.

"I killed dozens, maybe hundreds—with my words. It was after the war, during the People's Courts, when the fascist leadership went before our socialist judges. It took no courage, Risa. Nor would—" How can every topic be an electrified tangle of barbed wire? "The state would not consider it assassination, although I killed a prince regent. And a prime minister of our country. You would not want to write about it for school. I don't know if I could tell it all. Not to such a hopeful, such a pure face as yours."

"Daddy!"

I wipe at my face. "I'm sorry. This is—nothing works anymore, after prison. I'm like a faucet someone forgot to close."

One's older life is the strewn pile of dominoes, that fell the way they would fall. You think you're lining up hopes when you're young: a proud array, like soldiers. They're just pitiful blank bodies, face down, eventually.

Risa looks out the window. I am troubling her. As happens.

"What brave assassination have they taught you about in school?" I ask, when I can get hold of myself. "Tell me what you know, and I will see what I can add."

"It's of Reinhard Heydrich. The fascist. There were two Czech men who parachuted into Prague, and killed him. He was one of Hitler's favorites, and they managed to throw a grenade under his car."

"Yes."

"Operation Anthro-something."

"Anthropoid. *Chovekopodobna.*"

"Why does it have such a weird name?"

"Man-like; almost human. I don't know. I assume they meant it as a signal to the Czechoslovakian people, that they should resist, stand up to the fascists? Or maybe it was a secret name and had no meaning."

"I think it had a meaning, Daddy."

"Then it's the one I gave you. We had all sorts of such names, when I was in the resistance. We imagined—maybe this is something you can write, dear one—we imagined ourselves like actors on a stage; we didn't do something just to do it, we did it to show others."

"Show them what?"

I drank my tea, and for the first time since she opened my door I felt my heart slow to normal. A thought formed: *enjoy this*. During the prison years, I would have given an arm and an ear. I was talking to my daughter. She was *listening* to me, eagerly. We were together. "Are we talking specifically about assassinations?"

"Yes."

"That we were powerful."

"Did it work?"

"Did it work for the Czech men? What were their names?"

"I don't remember."

"Embarrassingly, I don't know either. Find out. History should not record just Heydrich's name, it should remember the heroes who stopped him. Did they show power, do you think?"

She takes a moment, she is genuinely thinking. I fall in love with her afresh in that instant, this girl whose welfare had kept me alive through the worst of what I suffered, but whose being had moved on while my vision was stuck at age 6. "They did. They succeeded in killing him. He was the highest ranking Nazi anyone ever assassinated. And, Daddy, *after*—they hid in a church, did you know that? The Nazis needed a whole division of men to find them and get them out. They shot at them, they blew the place up, they even flooded the whole church, did you know that? Turned pumps and hoses and tried to drown them. Still, the men inside shot at them when they came to arrest them."

I nodded. "It is extraordinary. Can I tell you what the men did, whose lives were in our hands after the war?"

She nods eagerly. She has a notepad, but it is closed. Her face is open; this she will remember, there is no need for notes.

Her eagerness makes me pause. *Nothing,* I was about to say. *They languished in prison, they came out to be jeered at and condemned by their own acts, and then they were executed.* But what is my point? What, as her father, am I trying to teach her? The men I killed with my words, they were Nazis, too, of a sort. Discredited men, who had discredited our nation. Some I knew personally. Our prime minister, who used to be rector of Sofia University—*my* university—and whose eminent studies in Germany had exposed him to 'scientific' Jew-hatred. Our minister of the interior, across whose wall spidered the map of new railways that he used me and other Jewish slaves to build. Whose railways were meant to carry us, in cattle cars, to Treblinka. Heads of the fascist army, and the secret service, and their undersecretaries, and the Tsar's brother, and…. Was my point that bad men die as cowards? It isn't true.

"Do you still play chess, like I taught you?" I finally ask.

She smiles. "I can beat everyone in my school." Then a flicker of frown. "Except maybe Elias. He's good at forcing moves. I've beaten him, but he's beaten me."

"That's very good. We'll play sometime. Would you play me?"

She hesitates.

"I'm guessing your mother told you, you weren't to come here often. Let's say, a month or two from now."

"Yes," she said.

I put my hands on my knees and breathe for a moment in wonder at my new lease on life. I have just decided I will be here, without ever acknowledging to myself I had decided the opposite. The horizon opens wider. I will put up with Dicho's lecheries and corruptions, I will not say a word; I will—how they said it on my release—keep my nose clean.

"Assassinations are crude acts," I finally say. "Imagine you are playing chess, like we used to, Risa. Suddenly you stand up and overthrow the board. You scream, 'I will never play with you again.' Have you shown power?"

"I did that all the time," she says.

"I know."

"I used to go crazy. You had to hold my wrists because I kept hitting you."

We are smiling at each other, and I think she's reassured, she's remembering the old me, the one who was strong enough to hold her, whose chest could take her blows.

"Did it change the next game?"

"No."

"Because I am your father. And the board, and the rules, and even your sense of what is meaningful about chess, came from me. Now I will tell you something important. In 1942, do you know what the newspapers looked like after Heydrich got assassinated? They did not say, 'board overturned, game can't go on, justice restored.' They did not show Czechoslovakia suddenly becoming independent. They showed—I'm doing this from memory, make sure I'm right, you know how to look up the old papers in the national library, a smart girl like you—a grand sweep of entranceway, with stairs. A coffin draped in a Nazi flag, soldiers at attention, before an immense crowd that was gathered behind. It was very like a set of chess pieces, with horses and pageantry and the military figures in uniform proud and gleaming. That is what it showed."

She is watching me.

"And the story, Risa. The story was of the Nazis sweeping the city and the countryside with tanks and infantry; they set fire to houses, they arrested and tortured, they drove thousands into prisons and graves, they crushed any gathering, they deported people into camps, they shot them in the street.

"The story they didn't tell, but was equally true, was of Heydrich's worst idea—that all the Jews should be killed—and how it kept rolling, Risa, rolled beyond his grave all the way through Germany and Austria and Czechoslovakia and into Poland and Lithuania and Latvia and Hungary and Yugoslavia and Greece and when it was everywhere else, this killing idea, this 'Final Solution' came to Bulgaria, too. In 1943, a year after Heydrich was killed, the rulers of our country were gripped by the plans of his dead hand. It took a miracle to save your uncles and your aunt, whom you've never met, but whom I grew up adoring."

"And you, Daddy, did it take a miracle to save you?"

I breathe for a moment. Did I feel saved? The truth was, in the war, it had fallen to me to break myself out of the labor camps. It had fallen on me to spring my oldest brother from the tobacco warehouse where he had been held, his knees seeping blood into the cement floor. The fists, the blows, the bone-breaking cold of the mountains where I served as a guerilla—it had all fallen on me. "It always takes a miracle."

Risa makes notes, then stops. She chews on the back of her pencil, staring down at the paper. She seems troubled.

I wait. Will she ask about the miracle it took? Will she ask about Baruch, who saw the way things were going here after the war, and took the rest of the family to Israel? Will she ask why I didn't go? Will she ask about the packages he sent, of medicines not available here, and how with that loving act he sealed my fate, because he did *not* ever mention that he worked in Israel for the Mossad (or maybe he didn't, maybe it was a Bulgarian mistake, how would I know and whom could I ever ask?).

After long moments she says, "I think we got away from the assassination."

I laugh out loud. It's an unfamiliar, a sort of awful sound, to tell the truth. "You're right. My point was, dearest, that assassinations are meant to show you have power—but everything depends on the aftermath. It shows you— clear as a thumbs up, thumbs down—if you had power—or if you were just expressing a rage of powerlessness."

Her brow is furrowed. "You either control the pieces on the board, or you're trying to upend them all and get out of the game, knowing you've lost," I clarify. "The men we killed, Risa—when they were gone, we picked up the next day as if they'd never existed. Heydrich—the Nazis picked up the next day as if *he'd* never died. That's the difference. So as brave as those men were who killed him, they didn't change anything. They just confirmed it."

She chews the pencil some more. I can see gears turning. A fantasy forms: Risa in some future where she grows up free, and happy, and loved, and inscribes with her pencil all the thoughts and dreams of a free and happy and loved human being. Her spirit is spared. It does not turn, as mine had, to fill notebooks in cribbed and broken lines in prison, notebooks and notebooks that are piled a half meter deep in my closet, and that no one will ever see.

"I think I'll call this essay 'the assassination game'," she says.

I want to hug her, but she is not done. She looks up at me, and I see that she sees me, and the humiliation and aching regret, and shame, and joy and vindication are all one feeling, and it is so big I have to hide it by staring down into my tea cup, long since empty, as if its leaves contain the future.

She says, "And Daddy? Heydrich *is* dead, and so are the fascists you killed. And isn't the aftermath now?"

In those leaves I see Dicho, ungarrotted, and his crimes, unreported, and me, putting up with whatever I have to put up with, to live, to see this child grown. I have endured much worse things. In prison. In the labor camps. In seeing my entire country and its hopes, the hopes I believed in after the war and my brother did not, turned to this. I have seen the worst, and Risa is right.

We are here.

## Note

1    Impressed by Heydrich's dynamic leadership in the competition with officials of the Nazi party and the German state for the leading role in "solving" the "Jewish Question," Hermann Göring, the recognized deputy of Hitler in this matter, authorized Heydrich on January 24, 1939, to develop plans for a "solution to the Jewish Question" in the German Reich. On January 20, 1942, At the Wannsee Conference he presented plans, authorized by Hitler himself, to coordinate a European-wide "Final Solution of the Jewish Question." He informed the participants that Hitler had both authorized the physical annihilation of the European Jews and had designated the SS—specifically the RSHA under Heydrich—to coordinate "Final Solution policy." Heydrich was so confident that his pacification program had succeeded that he flagrantly disregarded measures for his own security and traveled around Prague in an open vehicle. On May 27, 1942, as he traveled on a familiar route to the airport to fly to Hitler's headquarters, two Czech parachute agents succeeded in rolling a hand grenade under Heydrich's transport vehicle. Though not mortally wounded by the blast itself, the grenade splinters in his leg and lower back led to an infection that killed him on June 4, 1942. Both Hitler and Himmler mourned this most ruthless implementer of the "Final Solution." Hitler described Heydrich as "one of the best National Socialists, one of the staunchest defenders of the concept of the German Reich and one of the greatest opponents of all enemies of this Reich." On June 9, the day of Heydrich's state funeral in Berlin, Hitler ordered retaliatory measures against the Czech population.

# Buchenwald

RAFICQ ABDULLA

It's always winter here, the trees,
Close together huddling the darkness
With their silent pagan presences,
Witness our own befitting silence
With nothing to see, nothing to hear, nothing
To smell, no one to touch save in the imagination.
Determined to appease the dead,
We crunch the clinker as we walk between
The ghosts of razed buildings that hoarded
A frenzy of prisoners for tormenting.

No flies at this empty time of the year,
No demented midges to sublimate as we seek
Out the dead in us to talk to, not with words
But with the turmoil of the heart—who can speak of this?

**About the Photo:** View of a sign outside of Buchenwald which reads – To the Buchenwald Zoological Park.[1]

Who can accumulate the accident of lives that cry
Out to etch themselves in the strangers who try to roll
Back the present and weigh the air for unspent spirits?


(THE POEM IN ARABIC)


"معسكر الاعتقال "بوخنوالد
للشاعر رفيق عبد الل
)ترجمة راسل هارس ووليد غالي(
هنا يرفُضُ الشتاء أن ينتهي
وتلك الأشجار الكثيفة
،تحتضنُ الظّلامَ
وفي صمتٍ رهيبٍ لا دين له
.نَشهَدُ على صمتِنا اللائق
ونحن لا يوجد ما نَراه أو ما نَسمَعُه
ِما نَشَمُه أو من نَلمِسُه سوى في خيالِنا
عازمون على إرضاءِ الموتَ
نسحِقُ تحت أقدامِنا طريقًا من الرَّماد
بينما نسير بين أطلالِ مبانٍ
كانت في أصلها زنازينًا
.يُعَذَبَ فيها الأَسَى
،في هذا الشتاءِ يسود الهُدوء
لا ذُباب ولا براغيث تؤرَّقُنا
بينما نحاولُ مناقشةَ الموتَ
.في وجدانِنا ـــ بنبض القلبِ
تُرى من سَ وَ۞ي هذا الحديثَ عنّا ٍي
ومَن يفهمُ صُاخَ تلك الأرواح
التي تحاولُ أن تَحفرَ نفسَها
ـــ داخل حياةِ الغرباء
هم الذين يحاولونَ
تبديلَ الماضى بالحاضرِ وتقديرَ الهواءِ
.بحثًا عن الأرواحِ الحيَة


(ARABIC TRANSLATION BY RUSSELL HARRIS WITH WALID GHALI)

# Note

1 In 1938, as soon as the camp opened, Commandant Karl Otto Koch ordered the construction of a park area for the SS guards, just outside the camp fence. The park featured a birdhouse, a water basin, and a zoo for four bears and five monkeys. The bears were in full view of the prisoners, and there was also an elaborate falconry in another area outside the camp where the SS kept birds of prey.

Commanders' Order No. 56 dated 8th September 1938 (Extract):

> Buchenwald zoological gardens has been created in order to provide diversion and entertainment for the men in their leisure time and to show them the beauty and peculiarities of various animals which they will hardly be able to meet and observe in the wild.
>
> But we must also expect the visitor to be reasonable and fond of animals enough to refrain from anything that might not be good for the animals, cause harm to them or even compromise their health and habits. (...) In the meantime, I again received reports saying that SS men have tied the deer's horns to the fence and cut them loose only after a long while. Furthermore, it has been found that deer have been lured to the fence and tinfoil put in the mouth. In the future, I will find out the perpetrators of such loutish acts and have them reported to the SS Commander in Chief in order to have them punished for cruelty to animals.
>
> The Camp Commandant of Buchenwald Concentration Camp
>
> Signed by Koch
> SS-Standartenführer

## SS Photo, Auschwitz, 1944
JACQUELINE OSHEROW

Their backs are turned; we see no face,
unless you count the blurry one, in profile,
their children, too, just bundles, anonymous.

I'd no doubt find my double (shadowed eyes,
beak nose, high forehead, too gummy smile),
if their backs weren't turned. We see no face,

just coats and headscarves. But for the chimneys,
these might be any women facing exile
with their children and bundles, anonymous.

---

**About the Photo:** Jewish women and children who have been selected for death, walk in a line towards the gas chambers. Auschwitz, 1944.[1]

Today's have deserts, oceans, mountains to cross;
they too find soldiers, guns; they too stumble
while we, our backs turned, don't quite face

our part in this. We're charmed; we stay in place
or– if we so choose – travel at will
with our children, bundles. But who's anonymous?

We have our own borders and deportees
and, probably, right now, our own official
pulling children from their parents. He's our face
even with his back turned, anonymous

## Note

1    The "Auschwitz Album" is an album of photographs documenting the arrival, selection and
     processing of one or more transports of Jews from Subcarpathian Rus (Carpatho-Ukraine), then
     part of Hungary, that came to Auschwitz-Birkenau in the latter half of May, 1944. The album,
     which includes 193 photographs mounted on 56 pages, was taken by SS-Hauptscharführer
     Bernhardt Walter, head of the Auschwitz photographic laboratory known as the
     Erkennungsdienst [Identification Service] and his assistant, SS-Unterscharführer Ernst Hofmann.
     The album was produced as a presentation volume for the camp commandant. The photographs
     were arranged in the album by a prisoner named Myszkowski, who worked in the lab. He also
     decorated the volume and wrote captions for the pictures. The album was found after the
     liberation by Lili Jacob herself an Auschwitz survivor who appears in one of the photographs.
     The SS establishment also constructed one killing center in the concentration camp system.
     Auschwitz II, better known as Auschwitz-Birkenau, began killing operations in spring 1942.
     In Auschwitz-Birkenau, the SS had within the concentration camp system a killing center that
     had four gas chambers and that, at the height of the deportations, could kill up to 6,000 Jews
     each day.

# Words are Like Rivers

BRUCE BLACK

Back in the late 1980's, I drove a U-Haul truck with all my belongings from northern New Jersey west on Route 80 across Pennsylvania into Ohio to marry my future wife, and I knew that there was an Orthodox Jewish school, a yeshiva—the Telshe Yeshiva—in Cleveland because every year a blue box arrived in the mail containing colorful Hanukkah candles with a return envelope for a donation, and I knew the Hebrew Union College was located in Cincinnati, practically in Kentucky, where there were likely even fewer Jews than in Ohio.

I had family in Cleveland, long-lost cousins who we rarely spoke to, the silence a result of a family rift years ago, a lost love, one brother (my grandfather) who won the girl (my grandmother) and another brother who moved west to find a new bride and raise a family, and I'd heard of the great Abba Hillel Silver of Cleveland who served as rabbi of The Temple—Tifereth Israel for forty-six years, and who was one of the leading American Jews to support the founding of the state of Israel in 1948.

---

**About the Photo:** 26,000 people fill an arena to hear Father Coughlin "The Father of Hate Radio" speak in Cleveland, Ohio circa 1936.[1]

What I didn't know when I left New Jersey was how different it would feel to be a Jew in mid-Ohio or how vulnerable I would feel living far from my family and from New York bagels and delicatessens, how I'd feel as if I'd painted a yellow star on my back like a target or as if I'd hung a sign around my neck with the word "Jude" written in large black letters.

I remember going out to the mailbox in the afternoons to get the mail and often meeting one of my neighbors who told me that he and his wife were retired and that they enjoyed driving around the state visiting malls. One day he told me they had driven up to Cleveland and spent some time in "your people's" mall. "My people's mall?" "That's right, the mall in Beechwood," he said. Later, when I told my wife, she explained that Beachwood was a well-known Jewish neighborhood in Cleveland.

Now I can't help wondering if my neighbor as a boy might have attended the special event held in 1936 in a Cleveland arena where 26,000 people gathered to hear the "Father of Hate Radio" spew his venom against the Jews, and, if he had been there, if he'd taken with him memories of that day, and if he still heard the sound of Father Coughlin's voice in his head years later as he drove around the state visiting malls in the Jewish part of Cleveland or in whatever city he happened to find himself.

I lived in Ohio for two years until my wife and I decided to move to Philadelphia, the "city of brotherly love," so we could be closer to family. It's where Jews have been welcome since the early days of our country. And it was where the years that I spent in Ohio faded into memory and where the sound of my neighbor's voice, with all that his comment implied about Jews, faded into memory, too. I wrote a poem reflecting on all of this—

If you turn back the pages of Ohio's history, you can
hear ugly words like heeb and kike and traitor raging like
rivers and rattling the windows of the Cleveland arena
where some 26,000 people gathered in 1936 to hear
the "father of hate radio," the Reverend Charles E. Coughlin
spew his message of hatred against the Jews.

But if you listen closely, you can hear other words
rippling like Ohio's rivers down through the years,
words like freedom and peace and love, words spoken
by three Jewish students at Kent State—Allison
Krause, Sandra Scheuer, and Jeffrey Miller—who lost

their lives in a burst of gunfire on May 4th, 1971, not
because they were Jews but because they were
marching for peace, for *shalom,* a word you can still
hear echoing with their names across the campus.

You won't hear the words of Father Coughlin's message
any more in Ohio because they were drowned out by other
words, words that sing like rivers and bring
people together, unlike the venom-filled words of Father
Coughlin, meant to pull Christian and Jew apart, his
words of hatred powerless through the years against
words of hope, words like generosity, caring, and compassion.

Words are like rivers that feed our land, whether in
Ohio or anywhere else, nourishing green hills and snowy
valleys and inspiring all to melt swords into plowshares,
a torrent of words, filling ponds and lakes and
hearts with their healing power.

Words can give us the conviction to shape the land
we inhabit into the land our immigrant parents and
grandparents dreamed it could be when they
stepped off the ships or climbed over walls or fences
or swam across rivers, crossing borders to begin
a new life, drawn by the power—and the promise—
of words like freedom and peace and love.

## Note

1    Reverend Charles E. Coughlin (1891–1979) was a Canadian-born Roman Catholic priest and
radio celebrity based in the Detroit suburb of Royal Oak, Michigan. He broadcast populist,
anti-Communist, and antisemitic sermons every Sunday, and had more than ten million devoted
listeners at the peak of his popularity. By 1942, Coughlin's anti-Roosevelt and antisemitic
screeds had ended his radio career, but he remained a parish priest until his retirement in 1966.
Coughlin's hatred and suspicion of Jews may have been influenced by his clerical training in
the Basilian Order, a religious order he left in 1918. He frequently echoed the Basilian belief
that "usury"—the practice of charging interest on loans—was the source of the world's ills, and
he repeated the antisemitic lie that Jews were to blame for the practice. In a November 30,
1930 radio broadcast, Coughlin argued "that modern Shylocks [an antisemitic slur derived from
a character in Shakespeare's play The Merchant of Venice] have grown fat and wealthy, praised
and deified, because they have perpetuated the ancient crime of usury under a modern racket
of statesmanship." Throughout his career, he told listeners that Jews manipulated the economy,
railing against the "international bankers" and "money changers" of the world. In 16 weekly
installments of his publication Social Justice in 1938, Coughlin published The Protocols of the
Elders of Zion—an antisemitic pamphlet purportedly providing evidence of an international
Jewish conspiracy to control the world.

# *Regen aus Heiterem Himmel*/Rain from a Blue Sky

ERIN REDFERN

Tell me, mother, who is the prettiest girl?
That was me, daughter, during the war.

And mother, tell me who are your friends?
The *Helferinnen*, who sent and received messages.

Oh, mother, how could you, how could you be singing?
We sang constantly, our lungs charred and stinging.

Mother, what did you do when the officer wooed you?
I let him tipple me into the future (dear one, that's you).

And what made these stains on your mouth and hands?
Blueberries, my daughter, wild, coated with ash.

---

**About the Photo:** Solahutte Resort Near Auschwitz, SS and female auxiliary, typists, telegraph clerks, and secretaries called Helferinnen, which means "helpers."[1]

My own mother, what did you do when you wanted to weep?
Daughter, look closer: the bright sky wept for us.

And what did you do when the storm clouds came?
We laughed, and outran their heavenly strafe.

Mother, who made this place, so pleasant and safe?
They made it, whose hands bloom under black earth.

## Note

1    Solahutte, the photo's setting, is a "subcamp" of Auschwitz, built as a holiday resort for Nazis
     who were neither welcome nor safe in nearby towns in occupied Poland. Most of the
     resort—which included a sundeck, playing fields, a pool, and a sauna—was built by
     concentration camp inmates, who also did ongoing groundskeeping and housekeeping work.
     The photo is from the album of Karl Hoecker, an obersturmfuhrer or "senior storm leader" who
     was the adjutant to the commandant of Auschwitz. The album includes photos from the period
     of June–December, 1944.

# The Cigar Burning In Himmler's Hand
## ANDREW MCFADYEN-KETCHUM

"Take this cigar," Himmler said. "It too began
Its life as a seed cradled in the arms of its mother.
From her arms, it was plucked and stored until
It was its time to be planted in rows in the earth
With its brothers. Then time, our turning world.
Warmth. Water. The necessary nutrients,
And for reasons our 'science' still cannot discern,
It sprouted wings that lifted it out of the dark
Where it burst into light. There, again amongst
Its brothers, it was hammered into greater being
By the elements until it was severed at the base
And hung in rows above a fire that cured it
Of its blight, and what was once nothing but a seed

---

**About the Photo:** Reichsfuehrer-SS Heinrich Himmler smokes a cigar outside on the grass with
Reinhard Heydrich and two other officers during a trip to Estonia, 1941.[1]

Was harvested in bundles and transported by train
To the markets where it was bargained over
And inspected, turned this way and that
In the hands of men until agreements were reached
And a vast and important network of paperwork
Was authored and dated and signed, and the leaves
That once were seeds were again transported
By train to the rollers where they were sliced
Into strips by knives with its brothers
That were stirred together like ingredients
In a cauldron and rolled by hand in amarillo leaves,
Just another type of seed nourished for just another
Type of purpose until, we have, at last, this cigar."
Himmler paused then, turned his eyes to Heydrich,
The two young officers, the waters of the Baltic,
The grass waving on the hillside, the cornflowers,
The rooks ratcheting in the trees, the sky that soon
Would awaken with stars. Then he returned
His attentions to the cigar, brought it to his lips
And brought it to flame. "Transformation,"
He said then puffed once, twice, and regarded
The smoke that hung between them. *"This*
is the business we are in, my friends. Only *this."*

## Note

1    Heinrich Himmler was Reichsfuehrer-SS, head of the Gestapo and the Waffen-SS, and Minister
of the Interior of Nazi Germany from 1943 to 1945. Himmler was inspired by a combination of
fanatic racism and philosophical mysticism. He envisioned the creation of a pan-European
order of knighthood owing allegiance to the Fuehrer alone. When he was made Minister of the
Interior in 1943, he gained jurisdiction over the courts and the civil service as well. Himmler
ruthlessly utilized these powers to exploit Jews, Slavs, Gypsies and others for slave labor, to
shoot and gas millions of Jews, and to subject thousands to forced abortions, sterilization and
pseudo medical experimentation. Reinhard Heydrich was one of the main architects of the
"Final Solution." He was chief of the Reich Security Main Office, the SS and police agency
most directly concerned with implementing the Nazi plan to murder Jews of Europe during
World War II.

# Lubny, 1941

SUSANNA LANG

They told us, *Kirov Square,*
so I went, my youngest

in my arms and the older boy
smudge-faced

**About the Photo:** A young mother and her two children, Lubny mass execution. On October 16, 1941 over a thousand of the city's Jews, including women and children, were massacred on the outskirts of the city.[1]

by my side. Two jackets each,
hats pulled down over their ears.

The officers had said—
*warm clothes.*

* * * *

Who took this photograph?
Who recorded the moment before

they led us away?

* * * *

Of course I felt afraid
when the door of our house clicked shut

behind us. But I thought
for only a few months, a few years.

* * * *

Even now, mothers are pulling the doors shut
as they leave, their youngest

in their arms. They gather
at borders, where trains depart,

at the edge of the water:
everywhere men wait with guns.

* * * *

These ghosts,
they are your children now.

## Note

1    Jews were ordered to arrive in the village of Zasule for resettlement taking warm clothes and
     valuables. They gathered at the Kirov Square. The Jews were killed outside the city at Zasylskiy
     Ravine by SS-Sonderkommandos.

# Roma

BRUCE BOND

The hand along the margin belongs to a body beyond the frame.
It *belongs*, we say, as if it were possessed and so a thing to give away.
Behind the girl in the homemade dress, her hand on her brother
to coax him into the picture, the caravan tells us, they are travelers,
as hands are, when joyous or afraid. I cannot say she is among those
to suffer the chambers. Only that today a picture says what it cannot
to remember what it can. It is 1934 or 5. God knows. For a tyrant
regime meticulous with records, she is one of the race unworthy
of report. Hard to figure the number of wanderers led, by gunpoint,
into the final solution. To know the names of those who belonged
to no one nation. The untouched, unfettered. Who, one clear day
in a field at the edge of the village, entered the dark of the camera
that snipped the light that tied them, hand and body, to the world.

---

**About the Photo:** A group of Roma (Gypsy) women and children, circa 1934–39.[1]

## Note

1    It is not known precisely how many Roma were killed in the Holocaust. While exact figures or percentages cannot be ascertained, historians estimate that of slightly less than one million Roma believed to have been living in Europe before the war, the Nazis and their Axis partners killed up to 220,000. This photo was taken by photographer Jan Yoors (1922–1977). At the age of twelve, he left his parent's home in Belgium to seek out a group of Gypsies called the Lovara, who were camping on the outskirts of his town. When World War II began, Yoors decided to join the British Army. At the request of a British intelligence officer, he agreed to recruit Roma to assist Allied intelligence units, and together they worked to smuggle arms to the Resistance. They were arrested by the Gestapo in 1943, and Yoors was sentenced to death. He endured solitary confinement and six months of intermittent torture before being accidentally released a year later, due to a case of mistaken identity. Within a short time, though, he was again arrested. He was sent to the Miranda concentration camp (under Franco), where he remained until 1945. He learned then that the majority of his Roma family had been sent to Auschwitz, and had not survived. Yoors traveled throughout the world from the 1960s and early 1970s, and photographed extensively. He authored or provided photographs for several books, including The Gypsies (1967), The Gypsies of Spain (1974), and The Heroic Present (2004).

# Regarding the Pain of Others
## ALAN CATLIN

I've been thinking, lately, have for a long time,
about the pain of others. Not necessarily
about the Sontag book of the same name,
and how she suggested, with time and
over-exposure to ghastly images, that we
become desensitized. That the grotesque,
becomes somewhat ordinary, and that our
ability to empathize becomes stunted as if we,
subconsciously, lose interest.

**About the Photo:** Corpses piled up behind the crematorium in Buchenwald concentration camp,
1945.

I think, as well, of August Sander,
a German portrait taker between world wars,
whose mission in life was to catalog all types
of the Germanic people. How, eventually,
he was censored by the Nazis as his work
was not Aryan enough. Sander once said
that he did not deliberately make people look bad-
they did it to themselves. He must have recognized
that the Burghermeisters, in their impeccable
suits, the assiduous bureaucrats at their desks,
the self-important notaries, teachers, professors,
military men and the invincible young working
men, were identical in nature to the latter-day Nazis,
that only the time and place, that only the uniforms
would change.

And I wondered what kind of indifference?
What kind of perversion of imagination and design?
What kind of lack of basic human nature?
What kind of social pathology and lack of empathy
could create a situation that would become
this picture of men, stacked like cord wood,
as objects suitable only for burning?
These ruined men so far beyond pain and suffering,
is emblematic of what is evil in man. And there is
evil in man, make no mistake about that.
This image confirms it. Men are not objects
but human beings. It should never be necessary
to say this. Ever.

Sander noticed, early on in his career, the man
with the ledger, tabulating figures, awaiting
the next missive to arrive down the pneumatic
tube to his desk could easily be the civil servant
noting the numbers on the wrists of these starved
and worked to death, people, each placed in
their proper column, accounted for, written off.

I am so beyond pain thinking of this, I can no longer
make judgments. But I can weep at what I see.

# Good Girls

SARA LIPPMANN

When the photo appeared in the paper, our mother got bone still. We did not know why. We believed the man on the right was different from the man on the left. Two moustaches, but the man on the left was one of us. What was the worry? We were French. We did not yet understand the artifice of belonging. This was our tongue, our bread pressed against the pink flesh of our mouths softening to a paste we could swallow without sound. Our mother's coffee cup trembled in its saucer, but we did not yet know all the ways men would fail us. Once I'd called my sister, Simone, a two-faced rat, but mostly we got along, stayed out of trouble. At night, we pinned our hair into little rosettes. Our father might have died in his smoking chair, but we were not versed in the rules of betrayal. Surely, men meant to protect us would never throw us to wolves. This is not how government worked. That summer, upon word of the velodrome, we felt pride before horror. The 15th arrondissement! The famous cycling track! Home of the 1924 Olympics! Our mother sent us ahead, told

---

**About the Photo:** Philippe Pétain meeting Hitler in October 1940.[1]

us she'd follow. We believed this. She slipped a necklace into each of our shoes as collateral. Simone and I had each other. Lattice and steel arched over us like an industrial egg. Sure, there were rumblings, a feverish echo, but the place wasn't even full at first. It was flooded with light. You could picture a fencing match, the clang of swords, bicycles buzzing around with pointed caps in furious circles. We felt nation over faith until the smell took hold. There were so many people. Simone said, told you so. Told me what? Who were we to question authority? We wore smocked dresses and knee socks the color of city puddles. It was a temporary discomfort. In the distance we could feel the glimmering lights of the Eiffel Tower. Maybe they were stars. We couldn't see but in our minds we could see everything. There, in the sky! Some things are beyond imagination. So we waited and we believed. Hours accumulated. Our bellies cried into the hollow. Our cries dissolved into one deafening cry as men marched through in boots refusing food water toilet. Men turned up their noses, men spit at our feet, men called us cattle and vermin — in French. One man grabbed Simone by the waist. She was running her finger along a smudge of rubber tread, a vestige of cycling glory, or maybe it was blood or shit. By then, there was no telling. When she returned, she curled into my dress and I stroked her hair, curls limp. We were lightheaded with hunger. The room continued to swell until it began to empty, and still we waited, long after we lost our sense of smell, our sense of self of time, we were only bodies. We dreamt of profiteroles and sweet cream. Fields of lupine bloomed in our wet eyes. Simone took my wrist. Somewhere, out the window, lay the promise of bus to a train and a train to the countryside, where we vacationed that spring before papa died, and if we were good girls, did whatever's asked, the wolfman said, trust: it would carry us there.

## Note

1    State collaboration was sealed by the Montoire (Loir-et-Cher) interview in Hitler's train on October 24, 1940, during which Pétain, France's Prime Minister, and Hitler shook hands and agreed on cooperation between the two states. Organized by Pierre Laval, a strong proponent of collaboration, the interview and the handshake were photographed and exploited by Nazi propaganda to gain the support of the civilian population. On October 30, 1940, Pétain made state collaboration official, declaring on the radio: "I enter today on the path of collaboration." The Vichy government enacted a number of racial laws. In August 1940, laws against antisemitism in the media (the Marchandeau Act) were repealed, while the decree of September 5, 1943 denaturalized a number of French citizens, in particular Jews from Eastern Europe. The Statute on Jews excluded them from the civil administration. Vichy also enacted racial laws in its territories in North Africa.

# No One

MARILYN KALLET

No one talked about *les juifs*,
French antisemitism
When I was in school.
No mention of Vel d'Hiv,
More than 13,000 rounded up,
4000 children. No one said, Drancy,
Septfois, Auschwitz.
Gung-ho gendarmes.

---

**About the Photo:** Poster above the entrance of an antisemitic exposition called The Jew and France.

In September, 1941,
Parisians were on high alert
For sneaky Jews.
"*Comment reconnaitre le Juif?.*"
Get your antisemitic cue cards
At the Palais Berlitz!
Half-a-million visitors can't
Be wrong.
How to recognize a Jew?
The talons, the spidery greed!
In case you missed it, here's "Jewry
Feasting on the blood of
Our France."

The first I heard of this
Was at the dinner table in Paris,
Avenue du Parc Montsouris, 1966,
When Monsieur M. laughed about the day
The Paris police arrived at his factory
"and took away the Jews."
I was nineteen, a student boarder,
Kept my mouth shut, except to eat.

Palais Berlitz was only a palace if you
Loved Vichy France. Antisemitism
Is over, right? The Pope says
No. The graffiti on Eli Weisel's birthplace
Says no. Steve Bannon's crew
Laughs aloud. Jews
were "the enemy of the people" then.

I didn't taste antisemitism with my
croissant until I supped at Monsieur's table.
You don't have to be the Pope
to choke on today's hate-laced air.

# PART II ESSAY: A sociological perspective
## Thoughts about the Inhumanity of Humanity
ROB ROSENTHAL

It's an endlessly perplexing question: how could a species so capable of selfless sacrifice and mutual aid be so capable of individual cruelty and ruthless exploitation? How could the same species produce some individuals who run into a burning house to rescue strangers and others who would set that house on fire?

The inhumanity of humanity is accomplished, in the first place, through a literal belief in the inhumanity—the lack of humanness—of other humans. Those who are "othered" because of their race or their gender or their religion or their nationality—the list, sadly, goes on and on—can then be treated as disposable precisely because they are not considered human, not us. We do not treat those outside the group as we do those who seem like us.

The techniques of this othering may be nonverbal, as in the up and down assessment of the new kid's outfit which leaves no doubt where that kid stands, or in the prison clothes prisoners must wear to make clear their status. They are most obvious in the language we use, and in particular the way the grouping and collective dismissal of disparate individuals can be simultaneously signaled—heathens, kikes, fags, those people. All of these techniques, from the most subtle to the most obvious, share a framing that establishes not only difference but total exclusion. The other is not simply different, but so inferior as to have no claim on the common considerations due to those who belong.

Social psychologists have traced othering, in part, to humans' need to categorize—to simplify the enormous amount of information we are bombarded with every moment into discrete categories that orient us for understanding and action: is this dangerous, funny, pleasurable, deadly? We simply cannot function without this kind of simplification of the infinitely complex world we encounter. But the resulting simplifications in any given time and place are hardly "natural," the inevitable result of our need to categorize, since they vary so widely between times, nations, groups, and even individuals. Blue eyes may signify pleasure to some, danger to others, and carry no significance to still others. Racial identification through skin color may seem an obvious difference to some, but height might just as well be seen as a marker of in-group or out-group status. Social factors, created through historical accident, social narratives, elite manipulation, and so on, shape our categories, not only in determining which we think of as good or bad, but which are categories at all. Thus categorization may well be inevitable, but the categories themselves are so influenced by culture and history that there is no sense in speaking of them as natural.

Similarly it is sometimes argued that our capacity for cruelty is natural, that it's instinctual. In *Civilization and Its Discontents*, Freud wrote:

> ...men are not gentle creatures who want to be loved, and who at the most can defend themselves if they are attacked; they are, on the contrary, creatures among whose instinctual endowments is be reckoned a powerful share of aggressiveness. As a result, their neighbor is for them not only a potential helper or sexual object, but also someone who tempts them to satisfy their aggressiveness on him, to exploit his capacity for work without compensation, to use him sexually without his consent, to seize his possession, to humiliate him, to cause him pain, to torture and to kill him. Homo homini lupus [Man is a wolf to man]... [This aggressiveness] reveals man as a savage beast to whom consideration toward his own kind is something alien.

But if humans are capable of *both* great cruelty and great compassion—both a wolf to other humans and "a potential helper"—"human nature" cannot be a sufficient explanation for the Holocaust, nor for genocide in Rwanda, Kosovo, or Cambodia.

The question of nature versus nurture in human behavior has been debated for eons, but this much is clear: whatever our genetic disposition, whatever our "human nature," it must be extremely malleable, capable of taking extremely different forms under different conditions. The same "human nature" leads some to set the fire and others to risk their lives putting it out.

This then calls attention to the world we make. Some environments encourage, induce, even reward cruelty while others encourage, induce, and reward compassion. Some environments encourage the narrowest visions of who is a human and who is not, while others encourage the broadest notions of inclusion. Social scientists studying genocide note structural conditions which make such horrors more likely—political upheaval which threatens the status quo and ruling elites; war, particularly civil war; autocratic regimes—but as genocide researcher Timothy Williams and others have pointed out, such conditions are also present in societies that don't conduct genocide. While the overlapping configuration of several of these structural factors plays a role, far more important seems to be the ideology of the people involved, not as formal ideology, but in how we think about our place in the world and our relation to others. Where there is a tradition of inclusion embedded in both folk culture and formal institutions, genocide does not occur.

This, then, is our challenge: long before the troubles begin, before the pogroms begin, before the cleansing begins, we must nurture a world view that embraces difference as a strength, not a weakness or danger. Some are taller and some are shorter, but this is of no significance. The othering that makes genocide possible can only grow when designating anyone as outside the circle of humanity has already been tolerated or ignored.

# PART III

# Escape, Rescue, Resistance

## Prelude to Part III

The Danish Rescue / Heroes and the Valiant / Zionist Youth Movements / Warsaw Ghetto Uprising / Sobibor Revolt / Cultural Resistance / Partisans and Resistance Fighters / The Polish Home Army Resistance / The Ringelblum Archive

# Duckwitz

TIM SEIBLES

> *Georg Ferdinand Duckwitz, a diplomat of the Third Reich,*
> *secretly informed the Danish resistance of the plot to deport*
> *Danish Jews.*

Many things do not
work well, but I have
worked well without
wondering too much
about what I've been
told regarding the—
*The Jewish Question*
and how it might be

---

**About the Photo:** View of a Danish fishing boat that was used in the rescue of Jews during the occupation of Denmark.[1]

answered. I mean I
love The Fatherland
and you can't believe
everything you hear.

There are those who
always think the worst
when the news *could
be* made up, misun-
derstood, fake, mis-
taken. Who could
believe his country—
with everybody watch-
ing—would fall for
someone broken,
someone sick in the
mind: a person for
whom cruelty just
seems a simpler way.
The idea that *this* is

how it is, that my
work is done under
the governance of a
man whose hand I
should not, in good
conscience, ever take
makes me think of
myself with some
trepidation, makes
me want to do some
thing to wipe the news
off my face.

## Note

1    Driven by Thormod Larsen, this boat is the one now on display in the permanent exhibition of
     the United States Holocaust Memorial Museum. From September 20 into October 1943,
     approximately 7,200 Danish Jews escape to Sweden with the help of the Danish resistance
     movement and many individual Danish citizens. Resistance workers and sympathizers initially
     helped Jews move into hiding places throughout the country and from there to the coast;
     fishermen then ferried them to neutral Sweden. The rescue operation expanded to include

participation by the Danish police and the government. Over a period of about a month, some 7,200 Jews of the country's total Jewish population of 7,800 and 700 of their non-Jewish relatives traveled to safety in Sweden, which accepted the Danish refugees. Danish authorities, Jewish community leaders, and countless private citizens facilitated a massive operation to get Jews into hiding or into temporary sanctuaries. When German police began the roundup on the night of October 1, 1943, they found few Jews. In general, the Danish police authorities refused to cooperate, denying German police the right to enter Jewish homes by force, or simply overlooking Jews they found in hiding. Popular protests quickly came from various quarters such as churches, the Danish royal family, and various social and economic organizations. The Danish resistance, assisted by many ordinary Danish citizens, organized a partly coordinated, partly spontaneous rescue operation. Denmark was the only occupied country that actively resisted the Nazi regime's attempts to deport its Jewish citizens.

# Three Flowers

AMI KAYE

Her fingers trembled as she dressed them herself, sick from the weight of their innocence. Three children chosen to lure their parents from hiding. She knew they would never be seen again, but as headmistress she had to protect the remaining children in her care. Petal-soft faces turned her way when the Gestapo took them, and hammered her. The dread in their eyes lacerated her heart. Never again. *Never again.*

---

**About the Photo:** Jeanne Daman (center) poses with Jewish children under her care in the Nos Petits kindergarten. circa 1942.[1]

Conscience flared to resolve as she absorbed the atrocities around her: children torn from mothers; men battered and riven, eyes shocked with pain, bruises spreading under their ribs; people with stars on their chests rounded up, herded in sealed cattle cars, doomed to camps of hell where they were tortured and bereft under a broken sky, shot in the head or poisoned by gas. *She knew what lay ahead if she turned away.*

She bicycled all over the country to find refuge, guided the children to safety, nerves taut, listening for Nazi boots. Fear spilled into quivering throats and vandalized their sweet songs. Ominous shadows sliced through their night-mares. She ignored the warnings of her panicked mind and whisked them away as terror wove in and out through tall black trees, nipping at their heels. *No stopping, no turning back.*

*To rescue, to resist.*

Why, at the twisted commands of a monster or his automatons who massacred without question while a spineless world stood by? She grabbed the hands of human targets, became their shield. She led her charges through a trail of ashes and bones, agonized by their stolen futures, shattered lives. A wrong move or careless whisper meant certain death but three wilted flowers haunted her dreams, they became the voice in her head. *Stand firm against injustice; fight what is wrong.*

## Note

1    Jeanne Daman (later Scaglione) was a young Roman Catholic Belgian school teacher when the war began. After Jewish children were no longer permitted to attend regular public schools, she was approached and asked whether she would be willing to join the staff of Nos Petits, a Jewish kindergarten in Brussels. Jeanne was only 21 at the time. Not only did she respond positively, but she eventually became the headmistress of the school. When the deportation of Belgian Jews began in 1942, she helped find hiding places for 2,000 children. She also helped rescue many Jewish men by obtaining false papers for them. At the end of the war she became actively involved with the Belgian resistance transporting arms on her bike and providing intelligence for them. Immediately after the war she helped care for orphans, reunite families and raise funds for the United Jewish Appeal. She was honored for her work both by the king of Belgium and by Yad Vashem, in 1971 recognizing her as a Righteous Among the Nations.

# ichthus

JONATHAN KINSMAN

do you dream of the lion's mouth? its wet, yellow teeth;
wide, fleshy tongue; the darkness at the back of its throat?
the dust shaking beneath its paws; the terrible roar;
the crowd, chanting, singing; the flagellation of your heart?
angels walk in these dreams – grasp you tight by the shoulder;
say take the child and flee past the border, keep going.
don't look back, you'll only see the city burning,
licking at your heels. but these dreams are only dreams.
god does not call all of us to lay ourselves down in the street,
prostrate before the law while the prophets hang for words.
when the knock comes, answer. when the mob comes,
turn them back. carve the ichthus on your gatepost for a
fallen star of david. there are angels hiding in your walls,
beneath your floorboards, holding their breaths.

---

**About the Photo:** Pastors André Trocmé and Edouard Theis entertain themselves during their month
of imprisonment in the Saint-Paul d'Eyjeaux internment camp.[1]

## Note

1    Trocmé (right) plays the harmonica while Theis (left) reads a book. February 1943. André Pascal
     Trocmé (1901–1971), French Protestant pastor during the Second World War, played a central
     role in a regional effort to rescue Jews and other persecuted individuals.

     Le Chambon-sur-Lignon is one of a cluster of largely Protestant villages on the Plateau
     Vivarais-Lignon in the Haute-Loire region of France, where thousands of Jews and political
     refugees found shelter during the Second World War. The residents of these villages heeded the
     call of Pastors André Trocmé and Edouard Theis and other local leaders to extend aid to the
     persecuted even at the risk of endangering their own lives. It is estimated that 5,000 refugees,
     including 3,500 Jews, were aided by the people of the Plateau Vivarais-Lignon. Pastor André and
     Mme. Magda Trocmé and Pastor Edouard and Mme. Mildred Theis were among 34 residents of
     the Plateau Vivarais-Lignon who were later recognized by Yad Vashem as Righteous Among the
     Nations. Eventually, the entire population of the Plateau Vivarais-Lignon was so acknowledged.
     Ichthus is an image of a fish used as a symbol of Christianity.

# My Grandfather, a Refugee, Lined Up Outside the American Consulate in Marseilles

CHERYL J. FISH

They huddled. They waited. Outside the American Consulate in Marseilles, Place Felix-Baret, to beg for documents. Their hats on, their coats buttoned. Their stories already planted inside their heads. Will you grant me leave? Help me get out? I deserve to live. Some of them have husbands, wives, children, some are alone. They whispered on the street or stayed silent with hands in pockets. They didn't push. Some knew the name, (Hiram) Harry Bingham. He disobeyed orders from Washington. The one with the ear, the heart. He worked with Varian Fry from the Emergency Rescue Committee.

Bingham was 37, the Vice Counsel who chose to break the law. He did it for that author Lion Feuchtwanger, sheltered him in his own home and the writer overheard Harry arguing on the phone with his superiors. He falsified documents and issued visas well beyond the quota.

---

**About the Photo:** About the Photo: View from above of refugees lined up outside the American consulate in Marseilles. 1940–41.[1]

What about a humble house painter? My grandfather was one of those waiting. He came back each day, afraid to show fear, but his hands trembled even before he came to France. He thought about how he messed up the outlines of the stencils he was known for, he and his father and brother, for mimicking wood paneling on their walls, the grain and design their calling card. As they waited on the sidewalk they heard about camps in France, just the other day police from the Vichy, they summoned certain Jews to one called Les Milles. My grandfather Solomon Jacobs was young and strong and forceful once he opened his mouth, but he wouldn't do much talking unless they asked.

They gathered outside the large wooden door of the consulate waiting for hours. I ask myself, did my grandfather ever sing to himself? Hum as he stood there, time passing maybe his close by neighbor hearing the sound escape. Later he would join a Yiddish chorus in New York City, his singing providing not only an escape, but pleasure and no doubt evoke memories.

"When he plays a beautiful and heartfelt
Jewish melody on his fiddle,
oh, Mama, everything feels so good"
(From *Oy Mame Bin Ikh Farlibt)*

He would sing in Yiddish in ways I couldn't understand that went beyond the language.

Did you dare to sing in anticipation of annihilation or escape? Not all of them even fit on the sidewalk, some stood across the street, but in the photos I've seen there is no sign of hysteria. Imagine if my grandfather hadn't gone. When we cleaned out his apartment years later, we saw postcards from his brother and sister who stayed behind in Poland. They wanted to know all about America and arrive there too someday. But they remained trapped within impossibility. They became puzzling objects of death unanswered, details of their lives unknown, stamps on the card from towns soon obliterated. Harry's deeds were also discovered belatedly by one of his sons going through his papers after his father's passing. Harry didn't share his heroism. We also have this photo, a document that validates.

Why did Bingham take the picture of the crowd from above? Was he on a balcony watching those he'd attempt to rescue from the Nazis or just looking out his window? Stretching his legs between processing those hopeful Jews who begged for the right papers? Did he consciously gather visual evidence?

Reflect on the randomness and ethics of history? In ten months, he'd help 2,500 of them. I doubt he saw himself as a fine art photographer although he saved gifted artists like Marc Chagall, became good friends with him. Lisette Model was an influential street photographer from that time, but she focused on the leisure class, the average French citizen out for a stroll or sitting on a bench, in a strange hat, making a face, on the promenade in Nice. She became the teacher of Diane Arbus, famous for her photos of grotesque and yet poignant individuals. What Bingham captured from above was the orderly queue, civilized desperation, a tender chaos he shepherded. Bless him!

What were the odds, the chances that your ancestor made it out? I don't think anyone thought of fine art photography when survival was at stake. I search for my grandfather among the crowd and try to get inside his head. Of course, he's just another hat and coat from that angle, a lucky man. He never wanted to speak of life from those times, his face went blank, his brow creased, but he had that option thanks to Harry and whatever power beyond our control that may have intervened.

## Note

1    The Emergency Rescue Committee (ERC) was established in New York in the summer of 1940 in the wake of the defeat of France and its acceptance of Hitler's terms for an armistice. Article 19 of the agreement committed the new French government under Marshal Philippe Petain to surrender on demand all refugees from the Greater German Reich. The members of the ERC feared for the lives of hundreds of anti-Nazi refugee intellectuals and artists, who had fled the Reich and were now trapped within the closed borders of Vichy France. For their emissary to France, the ERC selected Varian Fry, an editor for the Foreign Policy Association with ties to the International YMCA. This connection allowed Fry to secure a visa to France at a time when they were difficult to obtain, as well as give him a cover for his rescue work. By the time he was expelled from France on August 27, 1941, Fry had spent thirteen months in the country. He and his colleagues had spirited more than 1,500 refugees from France and provided support to 2,500 others. Among the refugees he saved were the artists Marc Chagall, Max Ernst, Andre Masson and Jacques Lipchitz; the writers Heinrich Mann, Lion Feuchtwanger and Franz Werfel; the scientists Otto Meyerhof and Jacques Hadamard; and the political scientist Hannah Arendt. Varian Fry was recognized by Yad Vashem as one of the Righteous Among the Nations in 1994. The photo was taken by Hiram (Harry) Bingham IV (1903-1988), Vice Consul at the US consulate in Marseilles from 1939 to 1941, who worked with American rescue committees to help save more than 2,500 Jews and political opponents of the Nazi regime who were caught in France after the country's defeat. Sympathetic to the plight of the refugees, who were being incarcerated in French concentration camps, Bingham developed contacts with members of the French resistance. Later he used these contacts to assist the rescue efforts of Varian Fry's Emergency Rescue Committee and Frank Bohn's American Federation of Labor committee. In violation of US State Department regulations, Bingham issued hundreds of visas beyond State Department quotas and falsified others to provide cover for individual refugees. The whole story of Bingham's involvement in the rescue of refugees from Nazi persecution was not revealed for many decades until his youngest son discovered a bundle of documents in a cupboard behind a chimney in the family home. In 2002 Bingham was given a posthumous award for "constructive dissent" by the American Foreign Service Association. It was presented by US Secretary of State Colin Powell.

# Street Inventory

LAUREN CAMP

We see for you imagined pigeons. Every day albas
and thick oaks. Children: their purpose to giggle and leap.
People talk as shadow and we see blooms.

We take time to cross the bridge. We do it
for you, our veils leading us, the click of our shoes
placed, then lifted.

While we walk in light and return in light, we see for you
the shape of the light
so we can explain its tremble, remind how it switches.

We walk past tired women in a storefront.
They knead and bruise
small lumps of dough. Allow the bread

**About the Photo:** Muslim Rescuers in Sarajevo — Zejneba Hardaga (far right) with her sister-in-law (far left).[1]

to soft or crisp: a bounty. We smell the yeast for you.
What we don't see we stumble through.
Around the corner, the city will fall asleep in the long cloth

of night. We won't see those minutes
like knives. At dusk, a lessening. At our door, we move inside—
to you. The street is how we go

and we enter and hang up
the shape of north. The smell of autumn.
Tuning the radio through its bumps, we hear and you hear

the outrage. It spreads. So we repeat where we went
if you want us to repeat it.
We see for you the pleasure

of distance. Houses. What is unwavering?
Here is the wind. An hour with air. What landscape is.
Touch it. We brought it for you.

## Note

1    In April 1941 when the Germans invaded Yugoslavia, Sarajevo was bombed from the air. The home of the Kavilio family was destroyed. They had fled to the hills when the bombing began, and were now without a home. As they were walking to the family factory, they met Mustafa Hardaga, a Muslim friend who was the owner of the factory building. He immediately offered them to stay at his house. The Hardagas were observant Muslims. The household included Mustafa and his wife Zejneba, and his brother Izet and wife Bachriya. The Kavilio family stayed with the Hardagas until Josef Kavilio was able to move his wife and children to Mostar, in an area under Italian control, where Jews were relatively safe. Kavilio himself stayed behind to liquidate his business. Eventually he was arrested and imprisoned by the Ustasa. Because of the heavy snow, the prisoners could not be transferred from Sarajevo to the infamous Jasenovac camp near Zagreb, where the Croatians systematically killed Serbs, Jews and Roma. Instead the prisoners were taken, with their legs chained, to clear the roads from snow. This is where Zejneba saw Kvilio. Kavilio later testified that he saw her standing at the street corner, her face traditionally veiled, watching the plight of their family friend with tears in her eyes. Undisturbed by the danger, she began to bring food to the prisoners. Josef Kavilio eventually managed to escape and returned to the Hardaga home. The family welcomed him warmly and nursed him back to health. The Gestapo headquarters were nearby, and the danger was immense. In his testimony Josef described the notices on the walls threatening those who would hide Serbs and Jews with the death penalty. Not wanting to endanger the Hardagas life, Josef decided to flee to Mostar and join his family. On January 29, 1984, Yad Vashem recognized Mustafa and Zejneba Hardaga, Izet and Bachriya Hardaga and Ahmed Sadik as Righteous Among the Nations. "Whoever saves the life of a person is as if he has saved the life of the whole of humankind." (The Q'uran)

## Chiune Sugihara and Family Outside the Japanese Consulate in Koenigsberg
CYRIL WONG

In an old photograph, Sugihara
smiles beside his Japanese family.
Two European soldiers flanking them
in protective parentheses
smile for the camera, hesitantly
but gratefully.

**About the Photo:** Depicted on this page, Chiune Sugihara, the Consul of Japan in Kovno (Kaunas). The photo for which this poem is titled and based is unavailable.[1]

Unbeknownst to any of them
or not, Sugihara's country
was beginning to invade Southeast Asia;
possibly in the period the film
had taken to develop.

This is not to speak
less of the visas he issued
for Jewish refugees
in Lithuania
and the Polish underground
to flee with their families.

This is only to speak
of the blazing, admirable light
of Sugihara's fiercely
modest grin,
which had nothing to do
with the blood-
red sun
rising to the heart of his nation's flag.

## Note

1    Chiune (Sempo) Sugihara (January 1, 1900–1986) was the first Japanese diplomat posted to
     Lithuania. In the summer of 1940, Jewish refugees from occupied Poland came to him with
     bogus visas for Curacao and other Dutch possessions in America. Sugihara decided to facilitate
     their escape from war-torn Europe. By the time Sugihara left Lithuania he had issued visas to
     2,140 persons. These visas also covered some 300 others, mostly children. Sugihara also
     exchanged information with members of the Polish underground in Lithuania and issued them
     visas for transit through Japan in 1940. Shortly before his death, Yad Vashem, the Holocaust
     Martyrs' and Heroes' Remembrance Authority in Israel, declared Sugihara "Righteous Among
     the Nations" for his aid to the refugees in Lithuania during World War II. To view poem-related
     photo go to USHMM, "Collections Search," 07643

# We Built a House

DINA ELENBOGEN

*Sarah Weil writes to Shraga Weil at the end of his life*

\* \* \* \*

We built a house out of everywhere
because nowhere was safe except the place
our eyes met—even as yours looked west to Budapest,
and mine gazed east toward the dream.

---

**About the Photo:** Shraga and Sarah Weil, members of the underground movement of Hungarian
Zionist youth, 1944.[1]

We lived in the places our fingers joined.
Your other hand forged documents
so *Juden* could move invisibly through cities.
My left hand sewed lead from your pencils

into the hems of our coats, *just in case.*
We built a house out of just in case.
We ran with blueprints in our mittens, back
and forth to Slovakia, until we were caught.

They thought they could keep us apart
in the Hungarian prison but we still had the insides of your pencils.
I will never forget the words we wrote, one at a time
on scraps of paper, the words we rolled into balls and left

on courtyard sills. When they took us
on separate strolls, I saw your face in the distance
as you unrolled my gift. The smile that only I understood
bloomed in the house we built of secrets.

Alone I imagined your hands,
the lives you saved with your signature.
When I heard stories of others with yellow stars
my nights were the color of ash.

* * * *

We believed the sea would free us
as we sailed toward Palestine. We built
a house of water in our ship of orphans.
When we were captured again in Cyprus

your canvas held the blue of the Mediterranean.
For nine months you built structures
with the children, out of wooden blocks.

When we reached the shores of Tel-Aviv
a tent was already pitched for us on Kibbutz.
Our visions mingled with the soil that kept us.
Our hands, sticky from orange groves, were
always entwined. You called me

your muse and sketched faces of *halutzim*
the miracle of daily life, the way you once drew the faces of evil.
You made Hebrew signs and painted
pomegranates, phoenixes, and rams.

They built you a straw hut for your paintings.
Laughing, we called it the Louvre.
When you looked back, farther back than Europe,
you painted Jacob, Joseph and Abraham

who sacrificed his son.
I don't know when the colors
in Joseph's coat became black and white stripes.
The haunted face of the prisoner sits on the edge

of your canvas, My love. We built a house with our hands
our words and our silence. We built a house
of forgetting.

## Note

1    Born in Slovakia, Shraga (b.1918) and his wife Sarah (b. 1920) were members of the "Hashomer HaZair" youth movement. He studied arts at the Arts Academy of Prague until the beginning of WWII. During the war they were active members of the Hungarian resistance, mainly forging certificates and documents. Both were caught and put in prison. At the end of the war Shraga worked as a graphic designer of the Jewish Zionists center ("Haluzim") and Sarah, back in Hungary, integrated the movement's activities mainly rescuing Jewish youngsters and helping them move to Palestine. In 1947 both immigrated themselves and became members of Kibbutz Ha'ogen. Members of Zionist youth movements embraced leadership positions in ghetto resistance and partisan fighting organizations. Youth leaders of movements like Hashomer Hatzair, Dror, Betar, and He-Halutz such as Mordechai Anilewicz, Zivia Lubetkin, Yitzhak Zuckerman, Josef Kaplan, Frumka Plotnicka, Tosia Altman, and Samuel Breslaw were motivated by a sense of responsibility as local leaders, not only to their young movement members, but to the Jewish community as a whole. Before the war, their activities had been focused on Jewish youth training for immigration to Palestine. During the war their sense of responsibility and range of activities broadened. As part of their educational efforts, Zionist youth movements established "kibbutz" groups and underground schools in the ghettos. These youth movement leaders in turn became the leaders of the ghetto resistance and took the initiative in determining political and social action underground. Hebrew/German words used in the poem: halutzim (sing. halutz)=Jewish immigrant to Palestine esp. during interwar years Juden (sing. Jude)=Jews; the poet was able to have direct contact with Shraga and Sarah Weil's daughter to obtain details of their life which aided in the writing of this work.

# Witness

WENDY BRANDMARK

He could be my father. That man whose face I will never see, standing there, watching the flames.

I walk away from him to look at the rest of the exhibition, the photos of Bosnia and Rwanda. There are faces in these photos and bodies and children behind barbed wire. Downstairs in the museum we have dolls in old fashioned dresses and shards of pottery from Bavarian people in ancient times. You cannot go far from our town before you enter the forest, and if you keep going you reach the Czech border. From a distance the trees look feathery but their trunks are rough and strong like the bodies of hardened men.

She is an American artist traveling with the exhibition. I look at her name tag. When I ask where did her name come from because it does not sound American, she looks frightened. Just for a moment as if this were not now but another century. She says it is Polish, her grandfather's name.

**About the Photo:** A housing block burns during the suppression of the Warsaw ghetto uprising.[1]

146

She points to my metal badge. I tell her that now I am forestry commissioner but once I worked in the trees, climbing and cutting so others could grow. Some of those feathery trees are my planting, my children brushing against me, rows and rows of them, like young soldiers marching.

'That must have been scary,' she says. 'Knowing you could fall so far.'

'I felt safe up in the trees.' Where no one can find me.

'So you're fearless.'

'When the summer is dry, I'm afraid of fire,' I say.

Something else I fear, that the man in the photo will turn his head, and I will see my father's face.

'Why did they have to burn the buildings down? So cruel to kill them like that,' she says.

'Some had gone into hiding. Maybe the building was empty.'

She looks at me as if I am trying to absolve the Nazis.

'They were heroes,' she says. 'They had no hope, but they would fight and fight.'

I look again at the photo and see the heads of streetlamps gazing down on him that soldier who could have been my father. I point to the traffic sign, the zigzag hanging from the streetcar wire. 'Like the finger of God. A judgement.'

'Where was God?' she says. She cannot look anymore. The fire has gone inside her, the windows like wild eyes, the iron balustrade like a skeleton in the flames, the hollow of the building like her own body.

In my dream the soldier turns around but I cannot see a face below his helmet. I put my hands where his face should be but there is nothing there. Nothing. And no sound, the burning building a silent movie behind him.

The next evening at the reception, she seeks me out. 'I wanted you to translate something I saw around here.' She scrolls her phone to show me a photo of our war memorial stone with the words: 'Den Toten zur Ehr, den Lebenden zur Lehr'.

Why choose me?

'It means we must learn from the war,' I say.

'What did you learn?' she asks, and I wonder if she knows about the grave in the forest. Or the photos taken in our train station of Jews brought here after the war to recover themselves.

'I was born at the end of it all. So I am like you.'

I think she wants to ask me about my father so I say that he died in the war, in Russia he fell somewhere. I don't tell her that he was in Warsaw, one of the soldiers dedicated to the murdering.

I tell her that I have always lived in the town, my parents too were born here. And their parents.

'How nice to have that history with no break,' she says. I see no bitterness in her face.

'And you?' I start to say.

'My grandparents all came over to America at the turn of the last century. The usual story.'

Then they were safe I think.

'I must do my greetings,' she says moving away. Because our town dignitaries are here: our mayor, the museum director, even the man whose family has owned the local Schloss for hundreds of years.

I turn back to the photo. Someone else watches him watch the burning. The photographer tries to capture all of it: the building in flames, smoke filling the night street. Is it really night or does the smoke make it so? I want to shout at the soldier, turn your head, turn your head now before he takes the photo, and then I will know for sure. But the roaring of the flames makes him deaf to the photographer who also yells for him to turn. Maybe the soldier doesn't even know that someone is taking his photo. That I am looking at him.

And then I hear them through the roaring. I hear them screaming. And it's no use saying the Jews were elsewhere.

# Note

1 From the Stroop Report. The original German caption reads: "Destruction of a housing block." German forces intended to liquidate the Warsaw ghetto beginning on April 19, 1943, the eve of the Jewish holiday of Passover. When SS and police units entered the ghetto that morning, the streets were deserted. Nearly all of the residents of the ghetto had gone into hiding, as the renewal of deportations of Jews to death camps triggered an armed uprising within the ghetto. Though vastly outnumbered and outgunned, individuals and small groups of Jews hid or fought the Germans for almost a month. The Stroop Report was an album prepared by SS Major General Juergen Stroop, commander of the German forces which liquidated the Warsaw ghetto, to document the suppression of the ghetto uprising Commissioned by Friedrich Wilhelm Krueger, Higher SS and Police Leader in Krakow, and bound in leather, the report was intended as a souvenir album for Heinrich Himmler to celebrate the hard-won victory, which took twenty days and 1,200 SS, Wehrmacht, and police troops to accomplish.

# Sobibor

BECKY TUCH

Seven months I am in this camp and for seven months I follow their instructions. For seven months I bow my head and for seven months I sort the clothes that come to us in piles every day. Where do the clothes come from? Why are naked Jews marched into showers never to return? Where is the child who wore this dress? For seven months I ask no questions. I close the lid of

---

**About the Photo:** Selma and Chaim Engel (center) pose with their child and two other couples in Odessa where they were living under the assumed name of Kriseck. circa May, 1945.[1]

my heart, snap shut my inner eye. For seven months I feel hours stretch by, lean and long with empty aching, and for seven months I tell myself that I am nothing, no one, no self, so that in this way I might survive.

Eight months here, I meet him. "Dance," the SS officers command us at night, sputtering and drunk. "Tanzen, Juden!" A strange man takes my hand. Eight months here and I am feeling his palm cupping my elbow, his beard bristling my cheek. Eight months and I am smelling the sweet sweat along his throat, blinking into the dimple on his chin. But how to open my eyes to this man, when I've already sealed them? How to find a window in my heart that has been latched shut? Stay away, I hear myself whisper. Eight months I am in this camp and I know the danger of soft feelings, how they weaken and kill.

Nine months I am in this camp and for nine months I am sorting clothes and for nine months they are taking Jews to the showers and for nine months we are starving and for nine months we are sleeping on burlap and suddenly, in this ninth month, the fever finds me. Typhoid. My legs quiver. My head spins. Fever burns hot then cold. Nine months here and I am ready to die.

Would you believe, then, that I do not?

Nine months here and he finds me again, this man with the chin dimple, with earlobes swirled in white peach fuzz. *Selma,* he says to me, this man. *Selma, rest.* Nine months here and I learn his name. Chaim. He carries my body, limp as a rag, to a hay pile behind our work shed. He presses cold water on my face. He holds my burning head in his lap, runs gaunt and calloused fingers through my scalp. Nine months in this camp and love has come, banging on my inner door, as dangerous and bright as hope.

Then, one day, a miracle. Ten months here and Russian soldiers arrive, necks thick with muscle, eyes hard as bullets. Prisoners of war, we are told. Jews, we are told. But with them in the camp with us, it is different. The air stirs. A slow tide pulls back. These men are prisoners like us but they have what we do not have, strength, power, knowledge of how to hold a gun, understanding of how to kill. Ten months here and the whispered word on everyone's lips is *Escape.* Ten months here and we are beginning, again, to believe.

Eleven months I am in this camp. And on the sixteenth night of the eleventh month I am saying to Chaim in the language he does not speak, as I am Dutch, and he is Polish, *Ik hou van jou.* I love you. And on this sixteenth night of the eleventh month I am saying to him, *Hier, dood ze hiermee*. In a language he does understand I am kissing him on his mouth. And I am putting the blade inside his hand. Here, I am saying to Chaim. When the fighting begins, kill them with this.

Seven months later, seven years, seven decades—they will be wanting to know how we did it. Weak from hunger and despair, sick with trauma and disease, all of us speaking so many different languages, how were we coming together to hatch the plans and break the walls of our imprisonment? Is it true 300 Jews escaped from Sobibor prison camp in 1943? Is it true the Jews cut the phone and electricity lines, stabbed an SS officer with an axe, shot guards with their own rifles? Is it true, Selma, Chaim that you and Chaim ran through the barbed fence, dodged the land mines surrounding the camp, stormed into the woods, that you and Chaim hid together in a farm the remainder of the war? Selma, is it true that you went on, and on, and on, you and Chaim, moving away, having children, making lives? But how? How, they will want to know, did you possibly do it?

Yes, am saying, it is true, all of it. There is no secret I can be telling you about how. We simply did it. We did it because we had to. Sometimes someone is knocking on your door and sometimes you must be opening it.

## Note

1    Jewish prisoners at the Sobibor killing center started an armed revolt on October 14, 1943. About 300 escaped. SS functionaries and police units, with assistance from German military units, recapture about 100 and killed them. During the Sobibor prisoner uprising, Selma Wijnberg and Chaim Engel, who had fallen in love at the camp, escaped together. Two weeks later, hiding in a barn, Selma began a diary describing their escape, their fears in hiding, and their love for each other. They reached Odessa in the spring of 1945, where they boarded a ship for France. Eventually they returned to Holland, where they remained until immigrating to the United States in 1957.

# A man's arms may

## TC TOLBERT

Trick his shadow – may become the open chamber he longs to live inside –
Held in the lungs of another – what unforetold music may emerge
Even from the hair of a horse stretched between two bent ends of a Pernambuco stick and then
Rubbed against a dried and twisted selection of a young sheep's gut – it is 2019 and
Every day now the world's windows rattle – sunrise, that relentless bastard, still
Searches the dirt for what has the potential to explode – what cannot become louder larger
If only by eventually allowing itself to be slammed shut – perhaps this is another way of singing into
Every day's disappearance – enlarging what survives – without justification – here I am having
Never learned how to keep (this too the work of every beating body) time – what if we did not
Suspect the dead of going on somewhere without us – would we call our own names – if we knew
The very wind pushing through each fence, each concert hall was to be remembered
As another's expelled breath – silent – looking at you now, shaping sound strikes me as
Departure practice – lifting up from the shoulders a little – listening for the measure marked
*Tacet* – wave after wave expanding against one another – underneath loss lives touch –

---

**About the Photo:** Karel Ancerl conducts the Theresienstadt orchestra, 1944.[1]

# Note

1    Karel Ancerl had been the conductor of the Prague Radio symphony. He survived the war and
     ultimately became the conductor of the Toronto symphony. The artistic activities in
     Theresienstadt (Terezin) not only served Nazi propaganda purposes. In the musicians'
     appearances, in their mentoring of newly arrived artists, and especially in their performances,
     one gets a sense not only of the solidarity of the musicians with their fellow prisoners, but also
     of the educational, cultural-political, and psychological mission of music at Theresienstadt. Just
     by refusing to accept their current situation, the musicians were giving a sign to the others.
     Music thus became a means of retaining the identities of both musician and listener. Music
     simultaneously served to promote survival and signified hope for a better world. (spiritual/
     cultural resistance). Precisely because of the extreme situation of the camp and the possibility of
     death, the interest in music at Theresienstadt underscores the metaphysical content of art.

# So Be It (Amen)

## CORTNEY LAMAR CHARLESTON

There's God in the sky above and there's God
in my hand, not with me as a staff this time
but as what makes a clear path for light
through the body of my enemy who would
prefer me even lower than slave, somewhere
in the earth underfoot, as quiet as a period
after a period after a period.

        Let me tell you
what I see: a soldier's boot at the edge of a sea
of his own making,  romantic to the eye.

---

**About the Photo:** Abba Kovner (back row, center) with members of the FPO in Vilna, day of
liberation circa July 13 1944.[1]

This is not the vision my creator showed me but
the vision I showed my creator; no word was said
so there was no          disagreement, no dissuasion.
I decided to shave off the hair above my lip
to draw the distinction between us I needed
to draw my weapon.

Insert your pharaoh,
your führer, your president or prime minister
here, in front of me.


The anatomy of a bullet
and the anatomy of me are not so dissimilar—
the casing cooling in in the mud is not unlike
the compassionate veneer that I left behind
in the ghetto as I threw myself into this belief
with enough momentum to be instantly fatal.

I admit justice is not my concern here, just us;
they consider us to be a plague, so I oblige.


## Note

1    Abba Kovner (1918–1988), a Zionist youth leader from Hashomer Hatzair, played a key role
in the founding of the United Partisan Organization, FPO (Fareynegte Partizaner
Organizatsye), in wartime Vilna. It was Kovner who coined the phrase, "Let us not go like
sheep to the slaughter," In his manifesto of December 1941, calling for Jewish armed
resistance against the Nazis. As the commander of the FPO during the liquidation of the Vilna
ghetto (September 1943), Kovner directed the escape of the Vilna underground into the
forests. For the next ten months he commanded a Jewish partisan unit in the Rudninkai
Forest. After liberation Kovner returned briefly to Vilna before turning his efforts to organizing
the Bricha (the movement of Jewish survivors from Eastern Europe to the West). Kovner, like
many former partisans, was possessed by the idea of revenge. To this end he helped found the
Nekama [Revenge] organization in postwar Lublin. Nekama members set as their primary
goal the poisoning of millions of German nationals by contaminating their water supply. But
as a fall back, they adopted a plan to poison several thousand former SS members
incarcerated in American POW camps. Nekama's plans were foiled when Kovner, who went
to Palestine to secure the poison, was arrested on his return trip to Europe in December 1945.
After spending four months in a military prison in Cairo, Kovner returned to Palestine and
settled on Kibbutz Ein Hahoresh with his wife and fellow Vilna partisan, Vitka Kempner.
"Better to fall as free fighters than to live by the mercy of the murderers. Arise! Arise with
your last breath!" In the decades following the Holocaust and the founding of Nakam, Kovner
settled in Israel, married Vitka Kempner, published poetry in Yiddish and Hebrew, was a
founding member of the Museum of the Jewish People, and was awarded several prizes for
his work and legacy, among them the Israel Prize.

# DAWN
## FABIENNE JOSAPHAT

**I**

I remember my name in my father's mouth
before the shattering of our lives. In the hollowness of night
I listened. The sharpness of those voices rouses me still
from the deep of sleep. They sound like the discordant song
of sirens in the broken shards of moonlight.
By dawn, I remember. And every day after.

**II**

Our uniforms have adapted to our bodies.
I stitch my memories under the sun of Ohrid,
in the leather of our holsters, in the lining of our boots.
The surface of this lake is a mirror drinking the sky.
I stitch more memories in the clouds.
The shore is ashes. The wind, a song of forgiveness.
Their voices have not scattered in it.

---

**About the Photo:** Commissar Jamila Kolonomos and 3 other resistance fighters on the banks of Lake Ohrid, shortly after the town's liberation. circa November 1944.[1]

## III

My dead won't let me forget.
I learn to remember through resistance.
I long to build hillside homes like these.
I want to gather those families at my table
and break bread, and mend their pieces.
Outside our window, the lake is a mirror
held up to the world as it contemplates itself.
Beyond it, hope is the certain light of sunrise.
I leave a window open facing east to let it in.


## Note

1    Jamila Andjela Kolonomos was born in 1922 and she was raised in the Jewish community of
     Monastir (Bitola), a city in the province of Macedonia in the Kingdom of Yugoslavia. Jews had
     lived in Monastir for two thousand years. On April 6, 1941, the Germans entered Yugoslavia and
     Greece. Monastir was quickly occupied first by the Germans, then by the Bulgarians, and
     antisemitic laws were put into effect immediately. By the winter of 1943, there were only a few
     armed units of the resistance, dispersed in small villages far from the cities. In September 1943,
     Jamila was appointed Commissar of Brigade 1. On October 30, 1944, she participated in the
     liberation of the town of Ohrid and later, with great difficulty, of Struga. Until the end of the war,
     Jamila and her fellow partisans knew little of what had happened to their family members, and
     nothing of the death camps. They returned to Monastir, moved into two houses at the city center,
     and founded the postwar Jewish Community of Monastir, they began to hear more details of what
     had transpired after the deportations to Monopol. Conditions in Monopol had been abysmal. The
     Jewish transports had received no food or water for three days, followed by inadequate food,
     continual inspections, and beatings. Along with additional Jews gathered from Skopje and Shtip,
     they had been sent to the Treblinka concentration camp in three transports. After the war, Jamila
     was recognized many times for merit and bravery shown in her wartime service. She became a
     leading official in many political, benevolent, and social associations, including the Alliance of
     Yugoslav Resistance, the Union for the Protection of Childhood of Macedonia, and the Alliance of
     Anti-Fascist Women of Macedonia. In addition, she served as a deputy in the Macedonian
     Assembly. In 1962, she was named Professor Emeritus in the Faculty of Philosophy, Department
     of Romance Philology at Sts. Cyril and Methodus University, in Skopje. She is the author of
     numerous articles on Judeo-Spanish (the language of the Sephardim) and the
     Yugoslav-Macedonian Resistance.

# Without Question

LOIS JONES

*If you could lick my heart, it would poison you.*

—Simcha Rotem (In Memoriam February 10, 1924–December 22, 2018)

No one can take away that summer at sixteen
when the grass in the meadow was so tall

---

**About the Photo:** Leah Hammerstein Silverstein and Simcha Rotem January, 1945.[1]

you disappeared between its walls. Nothing above
but the clouds, plush as a rabbi's eyebrow, drifting

in imaginary lands. It was easy to dream
and let the sun drowsy the landscape until it was time

to bring the cows home. The taste of their milk –
clover, iris. The red palms of the corn poppies opening wide.

You could have lived on the back of that twilight watching
the wind sough the trees. But when you closed your eyes

you saw the wild-eyed animal trapped beneath
the cat knife. You smelled the musty vaults of hunger.

\* \* \* \*

Aryan fair, no one believed you were one of us.
At the Ghetto's gate you begged them, speaking Yiddish,

and muttered prayers until they let you in. By then
the currency of a quarter million humans

had been crushed. The largest bones ground
to a fine powder and stirred into the Vistula River.

When you entered the ghost town, feathers flew
in the wind, bits of rags remained in empty rooms.

No one could know when you inched along the ashes,
the smoke burning your nostrils with its oblivion,

just how the light staggered you among the ruins.
You crept near the corpses *dear to you*. Imagined waiting

for dawn and the cold end of a bullet. You might be
the last Jew in the Ghetto. You might follow

the woman's voice that called to you, but disappeared
from the rubble every time you got near.

When you finally built enough forces
to rescue the rebels, you made your way through

the sewers. Sometimes waist-high. Sometimes you crawled
on your stomach through shit and tears. You saved

as many as you could. Drove them
to the singing green of the Lomianki Forest.

* * * *

I do not have any questions for you. The solution
is hidden in the secrets of the grass, vaulted

like weed through the bodies where land broke
open its flesh. Because a photograph remembers

the shadow above the temple, will catch
the swell of lights that rise off the ground

in the graveyard – it will dig up the silence
your brothers gave you, will hold the gunshots

and barking dogs and the branches of unwilling trees.
Memory shudders by like a passing train. The good

will not turn away. Some nocturne seeps out
from the flames and calls you back.

## Note

1    During the final phases of the Warsaw Ghetto Uprising, Jewish resistance fighter and member of
     the Jewish Fighting Organization (ZOB) Simcha Rotem one of the few who survived, smuggled
     survivors out of the burning ghetto through sewage tunnels. Then, he helped them hide in the
     forests. After the war Rotem moved to Mandatory Palestine and joined the Haganah. He fought
     in Israel's War of Independence. Leah Hammerstein Silverstein (born Lodzia Hamersztajn) was
     born in the Warsaw suburb of Praga in 1924. During her high school years she became
     involved in the Hashomer Hatzair socialist Zionist youth movement. During the Nazi
     occupation Lodzia and her family were forced into the Warsaw ghetto. Maintaining her youth
     movement connections, Lodzia joined the Hashomer kibbutz hachshara (collective) organized
     by Mordechai Anielewicz and Josef Kaplan. Living on false papers, Lodzia moved between
     legitimate jobs and underground activities in Krakow, Warsaw and Czestochowa. At the time of
     the Warsaw ghetto uprising in the spring of 1943, Lodzia was on the Aryan side of the city
     serving as a courier. After the war she continued her underground activity as a contact for the
     Bricha, helping Jews to move out of Poland along established routes to the West. Lodzia also
     began a course of study at the university in Lodz. She remained in Poland until 1949, when she
     emigrated to Israel.

# Untitled (Maroon Bramble Wicks, August 1944)

MARK TARDI

> *"the heavens aren't silent*
> *if you have them in you"*
>
> —Robert Rybicki

We're listening to the darkness in the leaves,
to the fragile inner sound

that contains silence or hope or

---

**About the Photo:** Members of the Zoska battalion of the Armia Krajowa in action during the 1944 Polish resistance uprising. August 1944.[1]

the inevitable laid before us, cruelly patient,
and no one dares smile.

The petty facts of time and weather
tell us nothing.

Neither bricks nor bramble.

Two-thirds of visible boots
will never be equal to two-and-a-half

rifles — like how a wound forms when

something's willfully unremembered,

another life snuffed out
by the edge of the frame.

(THE POEM IN POLISH)

## Bez tytułu (Bordowe knoty cierni, sierpien 1944 r.)

> "niebiosa nie milczą
> jesli je masz w sobie"
> —Robert Rybicki

Nasłuchujemy ciemnosci w lisciach,
kruchego dzwięku wewnątrz,

który zawiera ciszę lub nadzieję lub

to, co nieuniknione przed nami, okrutnie cierpliwe,
i nikt nie ma odwagi na usmiech.

Błahe fakty godziny i pogody
nic nie mówią.

Ani cegły czy ciernie.

Dwie trzecie wystających oficerek
nigdy nie dorównają dwóm i pół

karabinom — na przykład, gdy tworzy się rana, kiedy

cos celowo przestaje się pamiętać,

kolejne życie zduszone
przez krawędz ramki.

(POLISH TRANSLATION BY KATARZYNA SZUSTER-TARDI)

## Note

1    The Warsaw uprising began on August 1, 1944. Under orders from the Polish
     government-in-exile in London, the Polish Home Army (Armia Krajowa) began attacking the
     Germans numbering only 23,000 underarmed men, the Polish fighters, under the command of
     General Tadeusz Bor-Komorowski, faced a German force of tens of thousands of heavily armed
     troops. Most of the Poles were young people and some units included Jewish (In November
     1942, ZOB, the Jewish Fighting Organization officially became part of and subordinated its
     activities to the High Command of the Armia Krajowa) and non-Jewish members of the
     Communist-oriented Armia Ludowa (People's Army, formerly Gwardia Ludowa or People's
     Guard). On August 4, the Poles liberated several hundred Jewish prisoners from the Gestapo
     prison on Gesia Street. These Jews, who were mostly Greek and Hungarian, joined the Poles
     and fought alongside them. Polish civilians also helped the insurgents by providing first aid and
     organizing supplies and postal service. Within four days the fighting had spread to large parts of
     central Warsaw and some of the city's suburbs. The Germans regained control of city on
     October 2. Over 18,000 Polish fighters and 150,000 civilians were killed during the uprising,
     including several thousand Jews who had been in hiding following the liquidation of the ghetto.
     Warsaw's remaining inhabitants were expelled to nearby internment camps, sent as forced
     laborers to the Reich, or dispersed in the General Government. The Germans then razed those
     parts of the city not damaged in the fighting, destroying Warsaw in its entirety. Though they
     treated captured Home Army combatants as prisoners of war, the Germans sent thousands of
     captured Polish civilians to concentration camps in the Reich. 166,000 people lost their lives in
     the uprising, including perhaps as many as 17,000 Polish Jews who had either fought with the
     AK or had been discovered in hiding. The Polish Home Army was one of the largest resistance
     groups in Nazi-occupied Europe.

# Unearthed (The Ringelblum Archive)

AMY GERSTLER

*Everything depends upon who writes this history.*
So, when the enemy walled us inside our city,
confined us behind barricades and razor wire,
we stood up to fate and began gathering.
For prisoners facing erasure, this was one way
of praying. We were doomed, futureless historians,
lace-makers and bakers. Apprentices, plasterers
and bricklayers. We were Jews, but we could have
been you. So, we assembled and buried this archive
of lost lives, just as you'd do, beneath a ruined
school. Our reverse-archaeology revolt organized
and annotated, crammed into milk cans and tin
boxes. Because something of us had to survive.
Because to bear witness is to resist. So, pickaxes
in hand, we planted a record of what was being

**About the Photo:** The first 'Oyneg Shabbos' archive cache recovered from the ruins of the Warsaw Ghetto Sept. 1946.[1]

annihilated, what the lucky take for granted:
so-called 'ordinary life.' *Remember stuffed cabbage? The gap
toothed cap-seller? Braided bread, crust studded with poppy seeds?
Remember waiting for the streetcar in a light rain? Walnut
and hazelnut trees? Courtyards and forests? Only 6 months old,
she's a bright, verbal child who doesn't deserve to die.* Our
impossible losses. *Soup topped with chopped dill. Boiled
potatoes with sour cream. Women in coats and wool berets.*
Diaries, drawings and posters we also put in.
Watercolors. Photos, newspapers and poems. Tram
tickets and candy wrappers (still a bit sticky). *Remember
knishes filled with kasha, slathered with mustard?* Sermons?
Songs from labor camps? Food stamps, restaurant
menus? *Yes, we were Jews, but we could have been you...*

## Note

1    The "Oneg Shabbat Archive" (Oyneg Shabbos Archive): begun as an individual chronicle by
     Emanuel Ringelblum in October 1939, the archive grew into an organized underground
     operation with several dozen contributors after the sealing of the Warsaw ghetto in November
     1940. The workers of the archive faced constant danger. They collected an enormous range of
     material, including items from the underground press. The holdings of the archives were buried
     beneath buildings in the ghetto in three parts. After the war, two of the three caches of
     documents were recovered. The commitment to comprehensive documentation went hand in
     hand with another important commitment: postwar justice. The chroniclers of the Oneg Shabbat
     felt a responsibility to document; if they did not do this, then who would? "It must all be
     recorded with not a single fact omitted. And when the time comes – as it surely will – let the
     world read and know what the murderers have done." —From the Oneg Shabbat Archives; "one
     of the most important examples of cultural resistance in the history of mankind" Samuel Kassow,
     Charles Northam Professor of History, and Director of Jewish Studies Program, Trinity College.

# PART III ESSAY: An ethical perspective
## Moral Lessons of Remembering the Holocaust: A Muslim Response
MEHNAZ AFRIDI

> *Beware of confining yourself to a particular belief and*
> *denying all else, for much good would elude you –*
> *indeed, the knowledge of reality would elude you.*
> *Be in yourself a matter for all forms of belief, for God is*
> *too vast and tremendous to be restricted to one belief*
> *rather than another.*
>
> *Ibn Arabi*

The quote above inspires me to teach the Holocaust and the Jewish tradition as a Muslim. My work on the Holocaust as a Muslim has been challenging in many ways but the scars of the victims live within me, as the survivor's eyes are forever engraved in my soul and last but not least my moral duty to remember the Holocaust. What does it mean to remember the Holocaust as a non-Jew? And why is this a moral imperative to all humanity? We have heard debates ranging from Elie Wiesel to Theodore Adorno to Raul Hilbert to Giorgio Agamben and Yehuda Bauer about how to remember and what it means to remember within the remnants of the Holocaust. However, the impetus for my work, teaching and activism revolve around one moral and ethical question: How can we forget such an atrocity and deform our memories of such a human calamity especially if we are people of faith? In my case, a Muslim.

The word *deform* is significant, as it means that we remember in our own individual and collective ways the way things imprinted upon us over years of recollecting a certain memory in different ways. The *deforming* of memory can be dangerous and at times, disingenuous in light of the perpetuation of antisemitism, Holocaust denial and relativization in many Muslim communities. *Deforming* memories of the Holocaust has been a way to delegitimize the memory of survivors.

The combination "Muslims and the Holocaust" is a rare phrase, but I am tied to it like a knot that tugs at me as I reflect on how the traumatic event of the

Holocaust has reshaped my own formulation of history and ethics. The Holocaust reaches into the depths of racism, evil and the brutality of human-kind. It deepens the existential angst of the value of life, yet it urges the spirit to live to tell the story of the Holocaust. However, we repeat the same mistakes over and over again.

Many things went wrong during the Holocaust from which we can learn diverse ethical lessons but one of the most crucial lessons that we can learn from our own ethical responsibility is that most people failed to live out their *prima facie* moral duty to refrain from hurting others. Most people fell into the pit of politics that raised a platform of years on antisemitism. Most people fell into the abyss of ideology rather than a faith that may have compelled them to act and think differently. Islamic social teachings compel Muslims to save and protect all human beings and accept them even if they are different from one another: *"O mankind, indeed We have created you from male and female and made you peoples and tribes that you may know one another. Indeed, the most noble of you in the sight of Allah is the most righteous of you. Indeed, Allah is Knowing and Acquainted." – [49:13]* The Qur'an warns human beings of evil and being bystander in situations when you may even have to go against your own people, the bystander effect is not permitted within Islam rather action and justice. As it states: *O YOU who have attained to faith! Be ever steadfast in your devotion to God, bearing witness to the truth in all equity; and never let hatred of any-one lead you into the sin of deviating from justice. ... And remain conscious of God: verily, God is aware of all that you do. [5:8]* Would these crucial verses have stopped the bystander or the perpetrator? It is hard to say but where was there any faith-based thinking? Where was the compulsion of religious and ethical responsibility?

Stories of the rescue of Jews are lost to many in Holocaust Studies especially about Muslims that can exemplify that human beings and countries can indeed take ethical responsibility and apply their faith and traditional religious learning to saving and sheltering lives. Some stories of rescue are well-known, but others are buried because of the *deformed* memory of the past. It is in keeping with the moral lessons of the Holocaust and our ethical responsibility to remember the heroes and the victims of the Holocaust. Remembering is an act of passing on the moral lessons. For example, one of my Muslim heroes is Inayat Noor Khan who was a Muslim working for the British as an auxiliary. "[Khan] was a wartime British secret agent of Indian descent who was the first female radio operator sent into Nazi-occupied France by the Special Operations Executive (SOE). She was arrested and eventually executed by the Gestapo. Noor Inayat Khan was born in 1914 in Moscow to an Indian father and an American mother. She was a direct descendant of Tipu Sultan, the eighteenth-century Muslim ruler of Mysore. Khan's father was a musician and Sufi teacher. He moved his family first to London and then to Paris, where Khan was educated and later worked writing children's stories. Khan escaped to England after the fall of France and in November 1940 she joined the WAAF (Women's Auxiliary Air Force). In late 1942, she was recruited to join SOE as a radio operator. Although some of those who trained her were unsure about her suitability, in June 1943 she was flown to France to become the radio operator for the 'Prosper' resistance network in Paris, with the codename 'Madeleine.' Many members of the network were arrested shortly afterward, but she chose to remain in France and spent the summer moving from place to place, trying to send messages back to London while avoiding capture."[1]

As with many stories during the *Shoah*, many victims were betrayed, stories shared by many. It was thus with Khan; the mistrust of a French woman took Khan's life away:

> In October, Khan was betrayed by a French woman and arrested by the Gestapo. She had unwisely kept copies of all her secret signals and the Germans were able to use her radio to trick London into sending new agents—straight into the hands of the waiting Gestapo. Khan escaped from prison but was recaptured a few hours later. In November 1943, she was sent to Pforzheim prison in Germany, where she was kept in chains and in solitary confinement. Despite repeated torture, she refused to reveal any information. In September 1944, Khan and three other female SOE agents were transferred to Dachau concentration camp, where on September 13 they were shot.[2]

She too was a hero, murdered by the same killers as the Jews. She was my heroine as a Muslim woman as well. She fascinates me—it is her courage that I can look up to and remember the many heroes that rescued one another in a great time of turmoil and uncertainty. A Muslim who worked for the rescue for Jews, hoping someday that she could help the victims escape—instead, she became a victim with other Jews in the same camp.

So, how can we forget that these individuals braved their lives in the midst of murder and risked everything in the name of Islam? Islam and Judaism share the same moral lesson of humanity in their respective sacred texts:

"We ordained for the Children of Israel that if any one slew a person –
unless it be for murder or for spreading mischief in the land – it would
be as if he slew the whole people: and if any one saved a life, it would
be as if he saved the life of the whole people. Then although there came
to them Our messengers with clear signs, yet, even after that, many of
them continued to commit excesses in the land." (Qur'an 5:32)

"Whoever destroys a soul from Israel, the Scripture considers it as if he
destroyed an entire world. And whoever saves a life from Israel, the
Scripture considers it as if he saved an entire world." (Babylonian
Talmud, Sanhedrin 37a)

## Notes

1   "Noor Inayat Khan 1914–1944," BBC (2014), accessed May 9, 2016,
    http://www.bbc.co.uk/ history/historic_figures/inayat_khan_noor.shtml.
2   Ibid.

# PART IV
## Aftermath

## Prelude to Part IV

Liberation of Concentration Camp Prisoners / Refugees / DP (Displaced Persons) Camps / The "Exodus 1947" / The Nuremberg Trials / UN Vote to Partition Palestine

# 1945

LINDA PASTAN

When my clownish, mustached, free-
wheeling uncle, surrounded by his dozen
Chihuahuas and his curvaceous third wife,
entered the army as a sort of larkish gesture,
loving the drama of uniforms,
the way a woman's eyes turned
in his direction, the snap, the precision of salutes;
when this sometimes wayward uncle became
part of the division liberating the first Camps,
it was as though the technicolor world he had always
lived in faded in an instant to black and white,
and he was struck to his knees, as Saul
had been on the road to Damascus.
Not by God this time but by His inexplicable absence.

**About the Photo:** An American soldier walks through the gates of the Kaufering I (Landsberg) Dachau concentration camp on the day of liberation. Original Caption Reads, "Landsberg Atrocity: 7th U.S. Army Troops enter the smoking ruins of the Landsberg concentration camp before American forces captured the camp, German guards locked the prisoners in wooden huts and set fire to them. Some burned to death in the buildings. Others found strength to crawl out to die in the streets. Most prisoners were naked, but some had remnants of clothing on their charred bodies." April 27, 1945.

# After the Liberation of Mauthausen: A Testimony

JEAN NORDHAUS

(On Seeing a Photo of Survivors in a Barracks)

The eye goes first to the naked torso
skeletal ribs like bars of a xylophone
(though who could dance to such macabre music?)

then to the bare foot waving almost gaily
behind the ear of the hollow face in the foreground,
eyes, deep pits from which no gleam escapes

then to the others. Cut loose from the world,
they could be interchangeable with one another,
with the torturers, the rescuers, even the man

**About the Photo:** Survivors in a barracks after the liberation of Mauthausen. Photographer Ray Buch. Date, between May 5–10, 1945.

who took this picture—Sgt. Ray Buch,
U.S. Army engineers, 11th Armored,
first generation German-American—

* * * *

By the time you reached the camp, the guards
not shot or hanged had slipped away, the guns
were gathered, a rough order restored.

Forty-five years later, on a flickering screen,
beatified by age, you tell your story. This was your moment
and you were for the most part up to it.

* * * *

*Anything else?* the interviewer asks.

* * * *

You shift in your chair. You've seen the bodies of the dead
along the road, seen the light-starved human harps
sunning themselves before the barracks. *I was stricken—*

you say, *by...the genitalia. The genitals were the last things
to go. The women's ...nipples ... the men's penises & testicles...
the things needed to reproduce life were about normal.*

*That's the one thing I will never forget.* The body
wants to go on, wants to take up the music
of being, go on.

# Aftermath

MYRA SKLAREW

*Everything that happened is imprinted within my body*

—Aharon Appelfeld

Trauma, where do you live in us
when the killing is done?

How do we seal you into your container
that you may not consume us?

Leiser, you helped deliver your brother Benjamin
on the floor of an earthen stable.

---

**About the Photo:** Joseph Schleifstein, a four-year-old survivor of Buchenwald, sits on the running board of an UNRRA truck soon after the liberation of the camp.[1]

You buried him days later. After the war
when you stepped into the sea, it turned to blood.

And here is Josef, on the running board
of an UNRRA truck. What lives are packed

into this small body? What inexplicable memories
must go on being interpreted for the rest of his life?

How to reconcile hunger and darkness and separation?
And for you, Sam, the vanished language of childhood.

I walk the perimeter of a massacre pit
dug into the banks of the Smilga stream

where twenty-nine of my family came to their end.
I climb down into an excavated pit in the forest

of Ponar and find a nub of bone in my hand.
Shalom goes at night to the place of Rabin's

assassination, but the sounds of multiple footsteps
awaken the death march he witnessed as a child

in the Kovno Ghetto when 9000 walk toward the 9th Fort.
Yocheved, I try to remember what you told me:

I believed I had the right to live.
Or Josef's words: Hate destroys the hater.

## Note

1    Joseph Schleifstein (born Josef Janek Szlajfaztajn) is the son of Izrael and Esther Schleifstein. He
     was born on March 7, 1941 in Sandomierz, Poland during the German occupation. The family
     remained in Sandomierz through its existence as a ghetto, from June 1942 through January
     1943. After the liquidation of the ghetto the family was moved to Czestochowa, where Israel
     and Esther were presumably put to work in one of the HASAG factory camps. During this
     period Joseph was placed in hiding in the area. Israel was sent to work for the Letzium Work
     Camp in the Radom District working for a firm called Ralnik from October 1942 till September
     1943. He worked in Makashin, near Sandomierz, from September till December 1943; in a
     HASAG ammunition factory in Kielc from December 1943 to approximately November 1944;
     and for a short time in Czestochowa. In January 1945, when the HASAG camps were closed
     and their operations transferred to Germany, the Schleifsteins were deported to Germany. Esther

was sent to the Bergen-Belsen concentration camp. Izrael and Joseph were taken to Buchenwald and arrived on January 20, 1945. Izrael successfully passed the selection process by concealing Joseph in a large sack in which he carried his leather-working tools. The child could not remain concealed for long in the camp, but his life was spared, in part because the Germans valued Israel's craftsmanship and in part because they took a liking to the child. The SS guards came to treat Joseph as a camp mascot, and even had him appear at roll calls wearing a child-sized striped uniform. Despite this special treatment, Joseph remembers being lined-up for execution at one point and his father intervening at the last moment to save him. He also remembers being very sick during his imprisonment and living in a hospital for a time. Soon after their liberation in Buchenwald, Israel and Joseph were taken to Switzerland for medical treatment. Some months later they were reunited with Esther in Dachau, where they lived until emigrating to the U.S. in 1947. The United Nations Relief and Rehabilitation Administration (UNRRA) was an international relief agency, largely dominated by the United States but representing 44 nations. Founded in 1943, it became part of the United Nations in 1945, and it largely shut down operations in 1947.

# Flight

## M. MIRIAM HERRERA

> *In each generation, a person must envision herself*
> *as if she personally came forth from Egypt.*
>
> —Haggadah

I imagine you lining up in Shanghai,
this day waiting for rice, not death.
A charred tree limb, slouching on lines
to freight trains, boxcars, cattle cars.
Shedding mementos, clothes, shoes, jewelry, body hair,
modesty, kinship, longing—selfhood.
Alive to witness liberation, you appealed for refuge:
*"Palestine. Palestine or the crematorium."*
As of one mind, a multitude of orphans flooded the harbor
and hardened the gatekeeper's heart.

---

**About the Photo:** Jewish refugees line up to receive food provided by the American Jewish Joint
Distribution Committee (JDC) after the war. Shanghai, China, 1945–1946. Even in the midst of the war
years, the Allied powers anticipated that a refugee crisis would follow the defeat of Nazi Germany.

Winter clung to life.
Songless birds tucked crowns into plumage.
We prayed the worst was over when icicles lost their blades
and snowmelt watered the barrens,
aching to nudge awake the world. Adrift
in a land of forgetting, earth fell into random orbit.
For you, the sun yielded shadow and the moon, smoke.

We fixed our eyes skyward,
yearned to see wild geese flying in v-formation—
like trumpet choirs heralding redemption.
Spring gained a foothold, yet you nursed the urge for going.
Perhaps you wished for all to be mindful of
the ambivalent sky, clear of flash or whirlwind,
for you to catch a sovereign flight?

The wind cried out, *Look up!*
Your wings dusted off shame for good,
as ecstasy rushed through me.
I whispered
*May you reach the sanctuary of home*
*and remember the breath of ease,*
*the arms of safety.*
*May you find the gates of compassion—*
*open*

## Nastupiste

PATTY SEYBURN

Yes. I will remember Prague.
The platform where the children tread.
Some carry satchels in their arms.
A hat or scarf protects the head.

You cannot see their eyes, their gaze.
A girl or two looks toward the lens
remembering some wheres and whens,
the lightness of her younger days.

---

**About the Photo:** A transport of 200 Jewish children, fleeing postwar antisemitic violence in Poland, arrives at the Prague railroad station.[1]

What do they carry in their hearts?
Their faces wear the old concern.
Another train. Another station.
Future. They cannot return,
wiser than Lot's wife. We've come
that far, at least. The aftermath
of horror leaves them lost, displaced,
neither there nor here, their path

untread. Oh God of Awe and Dread,
of Remnants, satchels, bird and sky,
provide them with a meal, a book,
a ball, a pillow on a bed.

## Note

1    The children are on their way to displaced persons camps in the American-occupied zone of
Germany. Prague, Czechoslovakia, July 15, 1946. The colossal relief effort was expected to take
no longer than six months. Between May and December 1945, the military, along with civilian
rescue teams of the United Nations Relief and Rehabilitation Administration (UNRRA),
successfully repatriated more than six million DPs. But the army was ill-prepared to handle the
one million DPs, mostly from eastern Europe and including 50,000 Jews, who refused to return
to the lands where their families had been massacred and where antisemitism still ran rampant.
The Jewish DPs (known as the "Sh'erit ha-Pletah"—the "Surviving Remnant" a Hebrew term of
biblical origin) became long-term wards of UNRRA and the occupying forces, especially the
American and British armies. The often harsh treatment of these displaced persons between
April and August 1945 blighted the record of the United States and Britain in the months
following liberation. Sh'erit ha-Pletah gained popular currency through the efforts of an
American Army Jewish chaplain named Abraham Klausner. In June 1945, Klausner compiled
the first list of survivors and chose the term as its title. As the 25,000-name list expanded into a
six-volume registry of Jewish DPs, the name Sh'erit ha-Pletah gained wide acceptance.

# Newer Eyes

## GILI HAIMOVICH

Eyes first
I's first—
this is where the I is found first.
My eyes, I, lose themselves to the faded selves I see.
I'm caught in a grasp of air.
The disturbing sweetness of defeated bodies.
The stare at the unseen.
What can't be seen, can't be imagined, isn't it?
Yet, it calls out to your DNA.
What is left then?
Darkness, even of a pupil, the grasp of air.

**About the Photo:** Jewish refugees, part of the *Brihah* (Hebrew for "escape" the postwar mass flight of Jews from eastern Europe), in a crowded boxcar on the way to a displaced persons camp in the American occupation zone. Germany, 1945 or 1946.[1]

Eyes are the first
anchors to the You,
observers through the dusty lace of decades.
(Does it matter? Your grandpa came from there, the others. From your
father's side as well, Romania. Once a North American told you it didn't
happen there. Her conviction stunned you).

An eye that stares back at you
from a women's profile,
bold, inquisitive.
And later, the ones who plead,
and even later, the washed-out ones,
already routed into absence.

An elbow sticks-out, pops out at the observer,
as if cuddling in a spoon-like position.
But no,
it's lifted so it won't squash the one underneath.
Is it that even when it's already near, death holds deception?

Mocks the appearance of this kibbutz of cuddles,
the intimacy of exhaustion.

The eyes don't rest
on any of the details.
It's here where gazing is the opposite of resting.
Falling into the merge of I's.

I give my newer eyes,
my unheard voice,
leaving its mute traces on the page,
letting this paper-boat fly away from its Israeli-Palestine anchors
to the temple of intention,
the pumping beat of recollection.

The last grasp of air,
the opposite of grasping at straws.
This is the last to be noticed:
A few straws, the earth under,

in the shape of a little triangle,
almost like a tip of a Star of David,
or a badge of shame.
And dust in all.

The only free spot
from eyes, elbows, clothes, people, bodies.
It's not a breathing space
but where a photographer stood, looking.
A full circle is now complete.
And this,
*for you are dust*
*and to dust you shall return.*

(THE POEM IN HEBREW)

**גילי חיימוביץ'**
**עיניים חדשות יותר**

עֵינַיִם קוֹדֶם
הָאֲנִי קוֹדֶם -
שָׁם אֶפְשָׁר לִמְצֹא אוֹתוֹ רִאשׁוֹן.
הָעֵינַיִם שֶׁלִּי, אֲנִי, מְאַבְּדוֹת עַצְמָן אֶל מוּל הָאֲנִי הַדְּהוּיִּים הַנִּרְאִים לְמוּלִי.
אֲנִי אֲחוּזָה בְּנְשִׁימָה חֲטוּפָה.
הַמְּתִיקוּת הַמַּטְרִידָה שֶׁל גּוּפוֹת מוּבָסִים.
הַבְּהִיָּה אֶל הַבִּלְתִּי נִרְאָה.
מַה שֶׁאִי אֶפְשָׁר לִרְאוֹת, גַּם אִי אֶפְשָׁר לְדַמְיֵן, נָכוֹן?
וְעִם זֹאת, קוֹרֵא לְךָ אֶל הַדִי.אֶן.אֵי.
מַה נִשְׁאָר אִם כֵּן?
חֲשֵׁכָה, אֲפִילוּ שֶׁל אִישׁוֹנִים, נְשִׁימָה חֲטוּפָה.

עֵינַיִם קוֹדֶם,
עוֹגְנִים אֶל הַ-אַתְּ
צוֹפִים, צָפוֹת, מִבַּעַד לַתַּחֲרָה הַמְּאֻבֶּקֶת שֶׁל הַשָּׁנִים.
(הַאִם זֶה מְשַׁנֶּה? סָבָא שֶׁלְּךָ בָּא מִשָּׁם, הָאֲחֵרִים. מֵהַצַּד שֶׁל אַבָּא שֶׁלְּךָ
גַּם, רוֹמַנְיָה. פַּעַם צָפוֹן אֲמֶרִיקָאִית אַחַת אָמְרָה לָךְ שֶׁשָּׁם
זֶה לֹא קָרָה. נְחִישׁוּתָהּ הַדִּירָה אוֹתָךְ.)

עַיִן שֶׁבּוֹהָה בָּךְ חֲזָרָה
מִפְּרוֹפִיל שֶׁל אִישָׁה,
נוֹעֶזֶת, חַקְרָנִית.
וּלְאַחֲרֶיהָ, אֵלּוּ הַמִּתְחַנְּנוֹת
וְעוֹד אַחֲרֵיהֶן, הַדְּהוּיוֹת,
הַמּוּבָסוֹת כְּבָר אֶל הָאַיִן.

מַרְפֵּק בּוֹלֵט הַחוּצָה, קוֹפֵץ הַחוּצָה אֶל הַמִּתְבּוֹנֵן
כְּמוֹ בְּחִבּוּק כְּפִיּוֹת
אֲבָל לֹא,
הוּא מוּרָם כְּדֵי לֹא לְמַעֵךְ אֶת מִי שֶׁמִּתַּחַת.
הַאִם גַּם כְּשֶׁהוּא כְּבָר קָרוֹב הַמָּוֶת מוֹלִיךְ שׁוֹלָל?
לוֹעֵג לְמַרְאִית הָעַיִן הַזּוֹ שֶׁל קִבּוּץ הַחֲבוּקִים,
הָאִינְטִימִיּוּת שֶׁבַּתְּשִׁישׁוּת.

הָעֵינַיִם לֹא נָחוּת
עַל שׁוּם פְּרָט.
זֶה כָּאן שֶׁבָּהֶיָה הֲפוּכָה לִמְנוּחָה.
נוֹפֶלֶת לְתוֹךְ הָעִסָּה שֶׁל הָאֲנִי.

אֲנִי נוֹתֶנֶת אֶת הָעֵינַיִם הַחֲדָשׁוֹת יוֹתֵר שֶׁלִּי,
אֶת הַקּוֹל שֶׁלִּי הַבִּלְתִּי נִשְׁמַע,
הַמּוֹתִיר אֶת עִקְּבוֹתָיו הַדּוֹמְמִים עַל הַדַּף,
מַתִּירָה לְסִירַת הַנְּיָיר הַזּוֹ לָעוּף מֵעֵבֶר לְעוֹגְנֶיהָ בְּיִשְׂרָאֵל־פָּלַסְטִין
אֶל מִקְדָּשׁ הַהִתְכַּנְּנוּת,
הַדּוֹפֵק הַפּוֹעֵם שֶׁל הַזִּכָּרוֹן.

נְשִׁימָה חֲטוּפָה אַחֲרוֹנָה,
הַהֶפֶךְ מֵהֵאָחֵז בַּקַּשׁ.
זֶה הַפְּרָט הָאַחֲרוֹן לְהַבְחִין בּוֹ:
מְעַט קַשׁ, הָאֲדָמָה מִתַּחַת,
בְּצוּרָה שֶׁל מְשֻׁלָּשׁ קָטָן

כִּמְעַט כְּמוֹ קָצֶה שֶׁל מָגֵן דָּוִד
אוֹ טְלָאִי צָהֹב.
וְעָפָר בַּכֹּל.

הַמָּקוֹם הַיָּחִיד הַפָּנוּי
מֵעֵינַיִם, מַרְפְּקִים, בְּגָדִים, אֲנָשִׁים, גּוּפוֹת.
זֶה לֹא מִרְוַח נְשִׁימָה
אֶלָּא הַמָּקוֹם בּוֹ צַלָּם עָמַד, הִתְבּוֹנֵן.
הַמַּעְגָּל עַכְשָׁיו הוּשְׁלַם.
וְזֶה גַּם,
*כִּי עָפָר אַתָּה*
*וְאֶל עָפָר תָּשׁוּב.*

(HEBREW TRANSLATION BY THE AUTHOR)

# Note

1   Zionism (the movement to return to the Jewish homeland in what was then British-controlled Palestine) was perhaps the most incendiary question of the Jewish DP era. In increasing numbers from 1945–48, Jewish survivors, their nationalism heightened by lack of autonomy in the camps and having few destinations available, chose British-controlled Palestine as their most desired destination. The DPs became an influential force in the Zionist cause and in the political debate about the creation of a Jewish state. They condemned British barriers to open immigration to Palestine. Zionist youth groups instilled an affinity for Israel among the young. David Ben-Gurion, leader of the Jewish community in Palestine, visited DP camps several times in 1945 and 1946. His visits raised the DPs' morale and rallied them in support of a Jewish state. The Jewish Agency (the de facto Jewish authority in Palestine) and Jewish soldiers from the British Army's Jewish Brigade further consolidated the alliance between the DPs and the Zionists, often assisting illegal immigration attempts. Mass protests against British policy became common occurrences in the DP camps. After liberation, the Allies were prepared to repatriate Jewish displaced persons to their homes, but many DPs refused or felt unable to return. Truman alone could not raise restrictive US and British immigration quotas, but he did succeed in pressuring Great Britain into sponsoring the Anglo-American Committee of Inquiry. This bi-national delegation's suggestions included the admission of 100,000 Jewish DPs to Palestine. Britain's rejection of the report strengthened the resolve of many Jews to reach Palestine and, from 1945–48, the Brihah ("escape") organization moved more than 100,000 Jews past British patrols and illegally into Palestine.

# What Comes Next

SCOTT NADELSON

By the time he arrives at Babenhausen, stealing has become more habit than necessity. Not so at Budzyn, where he nicked tools from the airplane factory and sold them to Ukrainian guards for an extra bowl of soup and half a pound of bread. The additional food kept him strong enough to live out those final months, fevered but still able to work, until being transferred to the main camp at Majdanek days before the Russians appeared. And from them he stole socks and cigarettes and a pocketwatch he still carries in his coat, which he stole from an American civilian on the train to Frankfurt.

Clumsy as a boy, and awkward, with big feet and ears that stuck straight out from the sides of his head, he has since learned deftness and caution. If he is good at anything besides thievery, he has not discovered what. He was seventeen when Minsk fell, which, if he understands the dates correctly, will make him twenty-three late this year. People tell him he looks older, even now that he shaves

---

**About the Photo:** View of a street of the Babenhausen displaced persons camp.[1]

regularly, his hair grown back to a length he can comb, his cheeks no longer hollow. Only recently has he been willing to answer any question about his origins, or at least to answer honestly. He once had a stolen name, too, taken from a dead Polish machinist at the airplane factory, but now, whenever anyone asks, he forces himself to use the one he was given at birth: Semion Gurevitch.

Except the Semion he remembers, a mediocre student who enjoyed reading philosophy but struggled in mathematics, who planned, grudgingly, to follow his father into the textile business, is not the same one who huddles into his stolen coat, hat pulled low on his head, so no one is likely to remember him as he slips down the camp's central lane, its gravel and dirt dusted with snow. It feels strange still to walk freely, without fear of being shot, especially as Babenhausen differs little in appearance from Budzyn. Rows of barracks, guard stations, a muddy field, barbed wire still being removed. He hurries past the newer housing units with tin roofs, occupied by families, to the former stables where single DPs like himself sleep on bunks stacked three high. If he's caught, he won't be shot, but what will happen he doesn't know, so he ducks around the side of the women's dormitory, presses himself against rough stones, and waits until he's sure no one has followed.

Before entering, he checks the pocketwatch. It's just past eleven o'clock, a gray morning with moist air that chills the freshly shaven skin of his neck. Most residents are occupied with a visit from a distinguished guest Semion has never heard of, come to sell them dreams of a new life in Palestine. He caught a glimpse of an old man with wild white hair, too fleshy to trust. What does he want with Palestine anyway, a place he knows only from books his grandfather made him study in the year leading to his thirteenth birthday. It has a sea nearby, that much he remembers, but he has never learned to swim. Nor does he care for the sound of Hebrew, which some devout camp residents chant after meals. Above all, he can't imagine living anywhere without tin-roofed barracks and soldiers patrolling after dark.

When no one has passed for nearly five minutes, he eases open the tall wooden door just enough to slide through. The stench of hide and droppings and old straw fill his nose, though no horses have stood here for years; before the Jewish refugees arrived, the camp housed German prisoners held by the Americans, and before that, Soviets kept by the Germans. Others hate the smell, but Semion doesn't mind. It's preferable to the stink of the latrines beside his block in Budzyn, where guards drowned prisoners caught trying to escape, head-first in putrid water.

His eyes adjust slowly to the dimness, taking in clotheslines strung across the open space between bunks and wall, draped with dresses, blouses, cotton undergarments he shouldn't see. So instead he scans for items left behind. He doesn't know what he's looking for, or rather, he's looking for anything that propels him forward. He just needs something to grab and tuck into his pocket, to finger as he waits for his meals, or as he lies awake in his bunk deep into the night. Last week he found a silk handkerchief, the week before a pair of reading glasses. Eventually he sold these things, too, for a pouch of tobacco, a crumpled green bill. That it's wrong to take from those who have so little, he tries not contemplate, because what other choice does he have? Sneaking into soldiers' quarters would risk too much. Though the Americans are here to protect them, he hesitates to cross anyone with a rifle in reach.

Also, he suspects, a number of the refugees, those who managed to evacuate from Minsk and Kiev ahead of the invasion, who spent the last five years in relative comfort and safety, some in the Caucasus, others as far east as Kazakhstan, have held onto valuable items from their old lives: necklaces and rings, silver forks and menorahs, gold coins. So he eases open metal footlockers at the ends of each nearby bunk, runs his hand beneath wool skirts and more soft underthings, loose threads tickling his knuckles. In the first he finds a hand mirror, a simple one with wooden frame, too small to show his whole face, which, in any case, he has no desire to see. He drops the mirror into his pocket. In the second locker he comes up with nothing.

The third's hinges creak when he opens it. He pauses a moment, listens, hears nothing. At the bottom he feels a small box, with a velvet cover. The texture alone, reminding him of the shop in Minsk, a corner where his father kept bolts of his best fabric, releases a strange ripple of relief, as if this is what he's been searching for all along, and he pockets the box without opening it. He'll save it until he has enough light to examine it properly, and until then he'll savor the anticipation. But the excitement makes him careless, and he closes the locker too fast. This time the hinges squawk, the lid clatters. And the sound is followed by a voice, from the dormitory's far end. "You can stop now." It's husky and tired but clearly that of a young woman. She has spoken in Yiddish, and when he doesn't answer, she tries again in Russian. "You don't have to do it any more."

He understands both languages but stays quiet, crouching beside the locker. His fingers are still wrapped around the velvet box inside his coat.

"Work so hard, that is," the woman says, sticking now with Russian. He can't see her past a wall of clothes hanging from the nearest line. "You can rest now, a little."

He stands slowly. There's too much space between his head and the high roof, no nearby supports to hide him. If he moves, she might catch a glimpse of his face, or maybe just his silhouette, but enough to identify him to the soldiers who police the camp. He pulls the cap lower on his forehead.

"I'm resting now," the woman says. "I can't get up to talk. And calling out strains my voice. You may as well come closer."

He knows he should run, take his chance that she won't see. But her voice, low and gently hoarse, complements the velvet against his fingers. He pushes through the hanging clothes, lets one of the cotton garments—one meant to be snug against skin—brush over his face. She is in the second tier from the end, in the middle bunk. Her outline comes clear first, small lump of head surrounded by black hair not yet grown past her ears, jut of feet beneath a blanket, and between them a huge mound of belly overtopping both.

"It feels good to rest," she says, her lips wide and dry beneath deep-set eyes, dark as her heavy brows. "To prepare for whatever's next."

He assumes she's referring to the coming child, though the way she inflects the word "next" suggests something as yet unknown. He thinks he should ask how soon the baby will arrive, but instead, in a voice surprisingly clear given how little he's used it, he says, "The father?"

She shrugs, passes a slender hand in front of her face as if to brush away the thought. "I have to sleep now. And you should leave before the others return." Her eyes close, but then, as if remembering something important, she forces them back open. "But since you've made the effort. That is, if you've found something worthwhile."

He fishes the mirror out of one pocket and then, reluctantly, the velvet box from the other. She reaches out the same slender hand. This time he sees, past her wrist, dark marks that reveal the place she has been, one even worse than Budzyn. The mirror leaves his fingers, hovers over her face. The reflection of dark irises flash at him, and then wood and glass slide under the blanket, disappear beside that impossibly round belly.

"Save the other," she says. "For next time."

He stuffs the velvet box back into his coat, turns, and hurries out, into the cold.

## Note

1   For the Jews who survived the Holocaust, the end of World War II brought new challenges. Many could not or would not return to their former homelands, and options for legal immigration were limited. In spite of these difficulties, these Jewish survivors sought to rebuild their shattered lives by creating flourishing communities in displaced persons camps in Germany, Austria, and Italy. In an unparalleled six-year period between 1945 and 1951, European Jewish life was reborn in camps such as Babenhausen. Babenhausen was a medium-sized Jewish displaced persons (DP) camp in the Frankfurt district of the American zone of occupation in Germany. During World War II, it had been a camp for Soviet prisoners of war. After the war, the still meager barracks created inhospitable housing for the DPs. The dismal conditions of the camp were reported in a December 13, 1946, issue of the Eschwege DP camp newspaper, Undzer Hofenung [Our Hope]: "Housing conditions here [in Babenhausen] are horrible. They used to be stalls for the horses of the Third Reich; now they are homes for the surviving Jews. Jews did not want to leave the trains so as to have to move in here." The US Army used the camp immediately after the war to hold prisoners of war. Thus, the camp did not open to Jews until September 29, 1946, when a train bearing 1,000 Jewish refugees from the Soviet Union arrived. When 1,200 more arrived two days later, the new residents lobbied the Army's Office on Jewish Affairs to protest the camp's conditions. Nevertheless, the camp remained open, and quickly reached a population of 3,026. It became a substantial community that earned a visit from Zionist leader David Ben-Gurion in late 1946. The residents of Babenhausen DP camp founded a Talmud Torah (religious elementary school) as well as a secular school. Babenhausen DP camp closed on September 6, 1949.

# The Displaced

BARRY SEILER

We see them standing on the deck,
staring back at the old world,
seeing themselves off.
What they see
does not show on their faces.
We see them: the orphans, the elderly,
the widowed and the married,
in borrowed coats and shoes,
their names pinned to their chests
so we can say them when they arrive.

---

**About the Photo:** Displaced persons (DPs) line the decks of the General Black as it leaves the port of Bremerhaven.[1]

We wonder if they know
their destination.
We wonder if they know
what *Ship To Freedom* means.
But, really, all they know is this:
they are sailing elsewhere.
Elsewhere is all.

On the dock,
the departed congregate.
This is not the afterlife
they were promised.
This is not
the old understanding
as they understood it.
Where is it written
they must bear witness
as the ship sails off
and the living stare through them
at God knows what?
Where is it written they must pray,
swaying in place,
chanting the names
of abandoned things:
*tattered suitcase,*
*wind-blown hat,*
*gold pocket watch,*
*shoelace,*
*pocket comb?*

## Note

1    Dubbed the "Ship to Freedom" by its passengers, it brought 813 European DPs from eleven
     nations to the United States under the provisions of the newly enacted Displaced Persons' Act
     (June 25, 1948). These were the first DPs allowed to enter the United States under the new
     quota. The ship's departure from Bremerhaven was marked by speeches by US military and
     civilian leaders and by an army band concert. The Displaced Persons Act that approximately
     400,000 displaced persons could immigrate to the United States over and above quota
     restrictions. US officials issued around 80,000 of the DP visas to Jewish displaced persons.

# If You, Like I, Seek a Happy Diaspora

NOMI STONE

In the Book of Exodus, years
before Solomon's reign, God
reveals his name and his law.
Lord of history, nothing is outside
his hand: the rise of the fat,
gold sun, the season when
irises clog the grass. The future,
its tidal pasts. You asked me to write
about the Exodus, the ship sent

---

**About the Photo:** Passengers on board the Exodus 1947 refugee ship, which has just arrived at the Haifa port, peer out of cabin windows.[1]

back and each life sent on, until
the State saved them and rose
like a sun. When you invited me
to write this poem, did you know
I made my own exodus? When
you asked me to make my biography
more Jewish? I am Jewish, but
I know no ships, and instead I dread
the State. Darlings, this is America,
fat into the second millennia. I am
the eldest child of a Rabbi and lived
in North Africa. I ate the flesh
of forbidden animals from land
and sea, wanting to eat with not
just us. Who? Hush, it's true
I know best about others, and how
each self holds strangeness in it like
a flame, as the morning opens,
asking me to number what I hold
dear. My sister's daughter is named
Eve, she wears her hair in braids,
she likes dried cherries and fears
little, and when I look at her my
heart hurts like staring into the sun.
One day a man came in her school,
a school for the Jews, and wrote on our
walls, *so numerous* send them into the waves,
I remembered my name Naomi
the irises on the hills open like eyes *Do not
come any closer. Where you are standing
is holy ground*

## Note

1   The British forcibly returned the refugees to Europe. Haifa, Palestine, July 19, 1947. The Exodus
    1947 was a worn-out US-owned coastal freight passenger ship launched in 1928. The ship was
    to take part in one more event which ensured its place in history. Initially sold as scrap for
    slightly more than $8,000, the ship was acquired by the Hagana (an underground Jewish
    military organization). Hagana personnel arranged to dock the ship in Europe in order to
    transport Jews who sought to illegally immigrate into Palestine. In July 1947 in France, 4,500
    Jewish refugees from displaced persons camps in Germany boarded the "Exodus 1947" and
    attempted to sail (without permission to land) to Palestine, which was under British mandate.

The British intercepted the ship off the coast and forced it to anchor in Haifa, where British soldiers removed the Jewish refugees. After British authorities failed to force France to accept the refugees, the refugees were returned to DP camps in Germany. The plight of the "Exodus" passengers became a symbol of the struggle for open immigration into Palestine. Displaced persons in camps all over Europe protested vociferously and staged hunger strikes when they heard the news. Large protests erupted on both sides of the Atlantic. The ensuing public embarrassment for Britain played a significant role in the diplomatic swing of sympathy toward the Jews and the eventual recognition of a Jewish state in 1948.

# Letter from Nuremberg, October 2nd 1946

*Between November 20th 1945 and October 1st 1946, twenty-one individuals stood before the International Military Tribunal authorized by the 1943 Moscow Conference on War Criminals. Of the senior surviving Nazi leadership, only eleven were executed. The rest were sentenced to terms of life or twenty or fewer years, or fined. Most were released early. Many were given pensions from which to pay their fines.*

**About the Photo:** During the Nuremberg Trial, American guards maintain constant surveillance over the major Nazi war criminals in the prison attached to the Palace of Justice. Nuremberg, Germany, November 1945.[1]

When I shipped from Fort Maxey
Earlier this summer the Texas flatlands
Were decorated with fennel flowers
And spindle trees were rising in bloom.
Here in Nuremberg—I'll send photographs
But I don't know whether the 793rd
Mail pouch rules permit—late summer
Has draped away. Already, winter
Embattles October: rough rain, hail studs.
It made me think about the pigpen outback
Our Nebraska farm. I miss you and Grandma.
I hope you can send a new toothbrush,
And maybe a bar or two of that soap
That Mama says is fragrant with cowslip.
I could use something reminding of home.

Germans count everything. Yesterday a fierce
Argument from von Krosigk's keen lawyer.
Schwerin von Krosigk, handsome and erect,
Kaiser-appointed German Rhodes scholar;
Privilege oozing from each confident pore.
From the start to the end with Hitler.
Never shirked. These days of course innocent,
No blood on his hands he swears. *"I only
Signed checks."* The work of Finance Minister.
Ever his downpour of pride gave no pause.
It's a gift how to choose not to reckon.
But why never ask who paid the tab
For railway cattle cars unutterable?
How many murders are too many to count?
*"We did what we did because we had orders".*


Defendant after Defendant. Litanies of innocence. I thought
of red-haired Bug Miller. Bloviating Bug could boost a strike
                three hundred clamoring feet over the cobbled left

        fence at the Schuyler Diamond up the road from where
        you parsed a slider from vexing screwballs that plunged
                into cornfields past a rusted John Deere '34.

I remember pummeling Bug's fists off the blooded jaw
of Sammy Nightingale, the Jewish kid who fled Augsburg
                    to farm our back twenty acres. Afternoons we lugged

        fetid mulch and boulders out of ditches. *"He's a kike, you know, so he
        gets what he gets"*. That's what Bug knew. How do we learn not to see
                    Our neighbors? I'm assigned heroic work, guarding

Goering's double-locked door. He's fatter than pictures depict.
Fussy, too. Every week demanding special treatment. Usually
                    a fresh toothbrush. But refused nail clippers, to protect

        Tribunal safety, he resorts to teeth. Last night he intrigued
        our Mennonite name. *"You're one of us!"* he applauded.
                    Sometimes, he hums. I recognized Cole Porter.

The *Reichmarschall* has beautiful hands. He conducts as he sings.
I'm sure his daughter must love her father. *"You'd love my dear Edda!"*
                    I had a dream I fought. Our Schuyler cousins

        assembled for Easter feast, hearing yet again how Sammy's
        ancestors killed Our Savior Lord while sweet Cousin Edda
                    searched the ditches discovering gold fillings.


Grandpa, it wasn't six million. It was five million
Eight hundred and seventy-three thousand
And twenty-seven. Each number ledgered.
*Dead, killed, sickened, erased, lost*: lawyers
Navigate too many words. *Dead* was worst.
Far too easy. Try *boasted*, try *slaughtered*.
How many murders before counting stops?
The numbers are impressive. Exactitude
Has experts: Uncle Heinrich's accountant craft.
Yesterday we heard blooded testimony,
November 26th 1945:
*Sturmbannfuhrer* Wilhelm Hoettle recounted
A conversation he'd had with Eichmann
In Budapest in August '44:
*"Could we, please, settle on a number?"*

I don't know when my job here will end.
There's talk we'll be sent early back State-side.
I think about what it will take to find soil
Worth planting. It's important to count.
But which numbers more than others?
After last shift yesterday, I trafficked
Under brilliant sunlight that washes
Through the atrium canopy, snaring
Everything in memory's grip. I heard
Mutterings from behind double-locked doors.
Some wept. Some exclamations of relief
That condemned bodies could provide pleasure.
I heard vulgar sing-song tunes, and water
Splashing from canisters each prisoner kept:
Washing stained hands; brushing their teeth.

## Note

1    The International Military Tribunal and a series of later trials held at Nuremberg, Germany, were
     not focused on the Holocaust alone, as reflected in the range of criminal charges brought
     before these courts. After much debate, the IMT charged a token number of defendants selected
     to represent a cross-section of German diplomatic, economic, political, and military leadership.
     The Nuremberg defendants were symbolic; the individuals held legally accountable for the
     Holocaust were only a fraction of those involved in perpetrating Nazi crimes. Of the verdicts
     handed down, eleven were given the death penalty, three were acquitted, three were given life
     imprisonment and four were given imprisonment ranging from 10 to 20 years.

## A New Passover Prayer Before the Eating of the Korech (as commentary on the Nuremberg trials)

RICHARD MICHELSON

Between the petitions God hears, and then— O Supreme
Court of neither nine, nor three, but One— refuses to hear;
and the forever faithful, filing appeals like still passionate
law clerks, Hillel sits. Between the not now, and the when,
Hillel sits. Between his ancient, bitter Babylonian grandmother
and her democratic-socialist-twentieth–century-post-holocaust
descendants, Hillel sits. So tonight, let us approach our tables
like a jury of peers. Let us neither judge, nor fill our plates
with the dark sweet paste of regret. Let us follow our prayers
to the empty chair between the Angel of Things We Will
Never Know and the Angel of All We Must Never Forget.

---

**About the Photo:** The defendants listen as the prosecution begins introducing documents at the
International Military Tribunal trial of war criminals at Nuremberg. November 22, 1945.[1]

# Note

1    The range of Nazi crimes was vast and legal efforts to punish them often yielded only limited results. Still, the Nuremberg trials set important precedents. The IMT declared to the world that "following orders" was not a legitimate defense for criminal acts. The trials also rejected claims that heads of state should be exempt from prosecution. After World War II ended, the Allies established courts in each of their occupied zones in Germany to prosecute German officials for their role in the commission of war crimes, crimes against peace, and crimes against humanity. American military tribunals in Nuremberg, Germany, presided over 12 major proceedings against leading German industrialists, military figures, SS perpetrators, and others. Included among these Subsequent Nuremberg Trials was the Doctors Trial. Note: The Korech, is also known as the Hillel Sandwich, after the great Rabbi who combined the three foods to be eaten in a Biblical command into a "sandwich." In modern times this often consists of setting bitter herbs, and charoset—a mixture of sweet apples and nuts— between two shards of matzah.

# The Last Survivor
## LIA PRIPSTEIN-LANE

From behind a glass, an Israeli spring is indistinguishable from winter.

Binyamin adjusts his sweater for the umpteenth time, fingers caught in snagged loops of yarn. He remembered Tal said four o'clock but as he watches the stillness of the street below, he is no longer sure.

The stone path to the building is lost in overgrown shrubs. Not too long ago his neighbor Shaul Kamenetzki had tended these shrubs. His bald head glistened in the morning glare as he contemplated each tender branch before applying the sheers. There's a story Shaul once told Binyamin about Majdanek

---

**About the Photo:** UN Vote to partition Palestine, November 29, 1947.[1]

where he'd been a prisoner. The floor of the munitions factory where he'd worked had been littered with scraps of metal. One day, unobserved, Shaul picked up a scrap and smuggled it into the barracks. He curved and bent, scratching lines to resemble the veins of a leaf, like the leaves he remembered from his childhood forest. In Majdanek nothing grew but gravel and mud.

In a flash Binyamin sees the metal leaf, small and hard, as if it was *his* hand that had held it. Lately it happened often, a story flaring up in his mind in a vivid image, more vivid than his own memories. The story outlives its subject. And isn't that the idea of this TV interview, to eternalize his life, capture a memory like a bird in a cage?

At the sight of an approaching car Binyamin jerks up, the sudden movement shoots pain up his hip. At times he forgets his body is not what it used to be. It could be worse of course. Alzheimer's, dementia, there's no end to the woes of the old. What Hitler had left undone is finished off by time, that systematic killer not even the fittest among them can hope to escape.

The car passes by and Binyamin slumps back over his cane. It wasn't until yesterday, when his Filipino nurse had asked in her heavily accented Hebrew when his show would be aired, that he felt the onset of panic. His testimony would be viewed by hundreds, maybe thousands. Family, friends of family, former co-workers and strangers scrutinizing his every word. And he? He could barely remember the name of the program they were filming. History Talks or Talks About History.

Serves you right, his wife would have said, you should never have agreed to this. She herself had rarely spoken about the past and refused to be filmed, even for Spielberg's SHOA Foundation. She didn't want to remember Auschwitz, wishing their daughter to grow up free of her parents' pain. If anything, her silence had the opposite effect. Their daughter became a historian, writing her thesis about the short-lived family camp in Birkenau.

Binyamin squints at the ripened sun. The interviewer, Tal, suggested it was his duty to speak.

These days as child survivors are ageing, she said when they first spoke, it's important to hear from a living witness.

How dire the situation must be if they came to him, an inmate of an obscure labor camp where extermination had taken the more mundane forms of hunger, exhaustion, and disease. In the unofficial ranking of Holocaust suffering his was a lightweight case, a lesser survivor story.

Once, speaking in his grandson's class, Binyamin was asked by a girl if he'd been in Auschwitz. He disappointed her by saying he hadn't. Auschwitz was famous, and his camp was not.

A young woman emerges from his building. She's a new neighbor on the second floor but he doesn't know her name. His suburban neighborhood is changing as young families from Tel Aviv are taking over the flats of his deceased friends. The old grocery store on Kehilat Padova Street, named after the extinct Italian Jewry, is now a Mega Market. The park benches on Kehilat Kiev, where he and his wife had sat in the afternoons, were torn out for more road. There's new construction on Kehilat Warsaw and the senior club on Kehilat Lvov is replaced by a preschool.

The old generation gives way to the new. He can almost hear his wife's resigned sigh as she says it, but his feet push into the floor, wishing to strike roots in the hard tiles.

The young woman nimbly navigates her stroller through Shaul's forsaken shrubs. Her hair, tied in a ponytail, swooshes back and forth as she skips over the path. She looks like a kid, they all do. Twenty, thirty, forty, he can't tell age anymore. In his teens a few years difference seemed like a lot, now entire decades count for a variation. When did he grow so old? He can't remember. When his daughter was born or maybe his grandson. When his wife rented space at the Hilton for their fiftieth anniversary or when she died clutching the hospital sheets for a fistful of life. It is as if a sudden blade had severed his youth from his self, wiping off heretofore tangible sensations of running to catch a bus and biting into a firm apple.

Behind him on the coffee table is a thin notebook he had written a lifetime ago at his daughter's request.

So you don't forget, she said to him then.

How can I ever forget?

Yet memories, like people, have their life span. Binyamin never thought he'd forget the face of the allied soldier who had sobbed as he lowered him onto the stretcher or the name of the transit camp nurse, a Jewish American woman, who had spoon-fed him back to health. When he was well enough she gave him one sheet of paper. Write what you saw.

He had so much to say it seemed he'd need a million sheets, but in the end it all fit, years distilled to a handful of sentences, raw memory fossilized in a block of text.

The girl with the stroller vanishes behind a curve just as a young couple appears. With them is the real estate agent who handled Zalman's first floor apartment. The other day he knocked on Binyamin's door to offer his card.

Take advantage while the market is hot, he advised. Your children and grand-children will thank you.

The agent's hands move as fast as his mouth. He is pointing things out to the couple, urging them to buy while supply lasts. Suddenly he looks up and gestures at Binyamin's window. With the sun where it is, it is unlikely the agent can see him, still Binyamin backs away as if touched by the angel of death. Chills rage through him like drafts through an abandoned house.

The old are always cold. Zalman wore his wife's shawl for his last year of life. Seventeen years older than Binyamin, he had lost his first family in Treblinka. One day Binyamin found him rummaging through his apartment, knocking off books and emptying drawers on the bed. Zalman had been showing signs of dementia but that day he seemed perfectly lucid. He was searching for photographs, he said, of his children Rivka'le and Moshko, the ones he'd raised before the war.

When the nurse had him safely back in his chair Zalman confessed to Binyamin. He remembered his childhood, the games he had played with his brothers down to the candy wrappers they used to swap with the Poles. But his children, the boy and the girl he had last glimpsed on the deportation platform, Zalman could not remember their faces.

Find me a photograph, he begged, just one.

There were none. Nothing was left of the children. Nothing but names on a memorial wall.

Binyamin returns to the window. The agent is gone. From the lull of white-washed houses and unperturbed trees, Zalman's cry rises like an air raid siren. How can one forget his children? Yet Binyamin knows, one can forget anything. The mind, that unkind beast, has a will of its own. It chews and chews, spitting out some, digesting the rest, and in the end that which gets stuck to the teeth is of no great importance, like Shaul's metal leaf and Zalman's candy wrappers.

A van pulls up to the curb, "Channel 2" splashed across the doors. Tal climbs out. Her hair is an unnatural red and her pants are torn at the knee. Binyamin is aware of the latest fashion. Hayale Elkind, one floor below, was always complaining about her granddaughter's tattered attire.

In the ghetto we patched up the holes, now they pay extra for it.

He had seen the granddaughter recently when she came to finalize the sale of Hayale's apartment. She inherited her grandmother's pointy chin and lively eyes.

I wish we could keep everything, she said, offering him some of Hayale's things, but there isn't enough room.

Tal is giving directions to the driver while the cameraman gathers his equipment. In a few minutes they'd be here, and Binyamin would have to recite his stories with an air of authority as if he knows them still. And maybe that's all they need, a voice and a face. It's understandable. Their battle is important and pressing, against ignorance and indifference, against doubt and denial. What do they care for the fog in his head, for words lying dead in his notebook?

For the sake of the next generation, Binyamin reminds himself. But as he begins his slow advance to the front door, he wonders what, if anything, the next generation should learn. The past has no definite lessons and survivor stories, moving and heartbreaking as they are, cannot inoculate against evil.

Why should they care for our war when they have their own wars to fight? Binaymin's friend and chess partner, Boris Zuskind, didn't think the Holocaust should be singled out. He had spent the war years in a Nazi camp and the post war years in the Gulag. A graduate of comparative internment, he joked, baring a row of silver teeth. He had neither regrets nor self-pity. One life is no worse than another, he said during one of their last games. In the camp we had our moments too.

They set up their stands and wires and a lamp beaming white into Binyamin's eyes.

Too bright? the cameraman frets. Let me adjust.

He is the age of Binyamin's grandson, his Sephardic complexion traced to a place as far from Hitler as any Jew could hope to be. Yet here he is, fussing over Binyamin as if it is his story Binyamin carries inside of him. Indoctrinated, his wife called these kids, third generation survivors all.

While the cameraman works, Tal goes over the outline. We'll start with your childhood before the war - the town, your father's store. Then the Aryan laws, the ghetto, the separation from your mother and sisters. I'll ask you about daily routines at the camp. Tree felling, meals, nights in the barrack then your father's passing, the foreman saving your life.

She speaks slowly, arranging his past into a rawboned plot.

Just what's in there, Tal points to a copy of his notebook in her lap, and if you forget, I'll guide you through it.

The cameraman counts back. The interview begins.

Words come surprisingly easy. His father's store was patronized by Jews and gentiles, his sister's wedding attended by the entire town. Binyamin sees neither the store's display window nor his sister's white gown, only words he had put down in the notebook all those years before. He recites them verbatim, like prayers or poems, one word out of order and he wouldn't know how to go on.

When the Wehrmacht marched in, my father wasn't afraid. He remembered the Germans from the First World War and had great respect for them.

Tal nods her head reassuringly. The interview is on track. Already Binyamin recounts his arrival at the camp, stock footage of German whips and growling dogs supplanting the true horror of those first moments outside the cattle car.

Tal's fingers pinch the edge of the notebook, ready to turn the page. Something stirs in him, an image so real it gives him pause. Fingertips finding a small patch of hair on the back of a clean-shaven head. Whose head? Father's. But why would his hair be of such interest? Because by then that's all that was left, a smidgeon of life cut at the root.

Binyamin knows this to be true, but he struggles to reconstruct the setting. Darkness, cold, wooden harshness of the upper bunk. Little by little his mind fills in gaps: the sour smell of sweat and the sound of men's stifled breath that he knows to be the staples of barrack life.

That first night in the barrack, he says, I lay behind Father, my face to his back. It was then that I felt it, a patch of hair above his neck. The barber must have missed it.

Binyamin speaks of the significance of the discovery, what it meant to the boy on the bunk, and all the while Tal is flipping through pages, a puzzled frown on her face. She won't find it in that graveyard of words. This one is real, a memory he can feel in his heart.

Tal raises her hand. The camera clicks shut, and the cameraman jerks his head away from the lens.

I'm sorry, you must be tired, she says. Let's take a break.

Binyamin is outraged. Why did you stop filming? It's not in the notes because I just remembered it. I was watching your fingers and it sprung on me so to speak. I know you have your order…

It's not that, she looks at him like a doctor about to deliver bad news. It's just that, well, you said your hair had been shaved.

So?! In Auschwitz it was standard procedure…

He stumbles, the horror of his mistake overwhelms him. He wasn't in Auschwitz. His was a labor camp. They didn't shave hair, not at first. It was his wife's memory he was recounting, one of the few she had shared with him in detail. How she had combed her sister's hair with her fingers, probing what was left of their braids.

I'm sorry. It was my wife, not I, he admits.

It happens all the time, Tal rushes to reassure. They call it false memory.

She means well but his chest is tight with abasement.

They move his chair by an open window then go to the kitchen for water. He can hear the anxious clanking of dishes as they hunt for a glass.

The day is fading, clouds graying as sunlight drains from the sky. Binyamin shuts his eyes. From the swampland of memories something pushes to the fore, not so much a vision as a sensation: spring afternoon, light breeze, the fungi smell of growth. He's in the field, crouched in a group of men. They're on their way back from the woods though he can't say why they stopped where they did. Perhaps there's a head count or maybe the guard decided to give them a rest. Vogel, the nicer German, would sometimes do that.

Sharp knees drop in the soft earth, so lightweight they don't leave a mark. There's pain where stripped bones rub against joints, where the skin stretches to thin it is tearing. Already the breeze chills his stomach, his chest, his unprotected heart. Father is dead. His mother, his sister, everyone he'd ever known and loved. For all he knows he and these skeletons crouching beside him are all that's left of his kind.

He longs to surrender into the earth, lay his head in the grass, let his limbs fall where they would. The end will be quick. Vogel is a good shot.

His body sways but refuses to fall. Like a branch bound to an invisible trunk, he cannot help but stiffen his grip as the breeze intensifies.

He draws a breath and his ears fill with the resounding beat of his pulse.

It is spring. He is still here, still alive.

## Note

1    "Witness accounts of the momentous vote in 1947 describe the delegates' cars pulling up outside the gray building at Flushing Meadow, outside New York, on a cold November afternoon, the crowds gathered outside, an electric excitement inside. People all over the world listened to a live radio broadcast. The vote was to decide whether to partition the British Mandate territory of Palestine into two states, one for Jews and one for Arabs. To pass, the motion needed a two-thirds majority. The Jews were in favor, the Arabs opposed. Feverish

international lobbying by both sides had preceded the vote. A Brazilian diplomat, Oswaldo Aranha, presided over the meeting from a high table. Next to him was the secretary general, the Norwegian Trygve Lie.In front of them stood a glass water pitcher and microphones that looked like metallic hard-boiled eggs. Behind them was an enormous painting of the globe. The two men faced a wide semicircle of delegations with table signs, and the packed galleries according to an account written by the Zionist delegate David Horowitz. Footage of the vote, and the discussions that preceded it, was preserved by the Spielberg Jewish Film Archive and is available online. The grainy film still conveys the remarkable drama of that day. A roll call began. Each country's delegate shouted from the floor, 'Yes,' 'No,' or 'Absention.' When it was France's turn, the auditorium held its breath; most expected the French to abstain. When their delegate said 'Yes,' the Zionist supporters who filled the galleries erupted into cheers. The president rapped sharply for order and warned the public against demonstrations. Voting resumed. When it was over, the president rapped his gavel again and read out the tally: Thirty-three in favor, thirteen against, eleven abstentions. The motion had passed."

(from *Times of Israel* article, 11/28/2012 by Matti Friedman).

On 24 October 1945, at the end of World War II, the UN organization was established with the aim of preventing future wars. At its founding, the UN had 51 member states; there are now 193. The UN is the successor of the ineffective League of Nations.

"There is intense disagreement among historians and activists about events surrounding the establishment of Israel, and journalists and educators alike must take care in describing them or risk appearing to take sides in the historical and political disputes."

(for the record statement from the *NYT* related to its Learning Network article).

# PART IV ESSAY: An existential perspective
## Virtues in the Wake of Auschwitz
SAM FLEISCHACKER

Eighty years ago, my parents fled Germany to evade the clutches of a tyrant who was out to destroy all Jews. I heard often, growing up, about Germans who helped my parents as well as Germans who went along with Hitler. I have also often wondered what makes for the sort of person who goes along with evil regimes and what makes for the sort of person who opposes them; I wonder, in particular, which I would myself had been, had I lived in Nazi Germany — or in Stalin's Russia, or the antebellum South, or apartheid South Africa.

This question becomes more urgent in times when illiberal and populist movements come to power; when for example attacks on the free press occur, when opponents of those in power are labeled as traitors, when there are attempts to co-opt the judiciary. In any country in which circumstances like these arise, it becomes reasonable to ask oneself "At what point might fascist dictatorship, or genocide, become a real possibility here, and what should I be doing to try to prevent that possibility?"

Let me note that I think it is a serious mistake to refuse to countenance comparisons to the Holocaust, or to use the slogan "Never again!" as a shield against recognizing that horrors very like the Holocaust have happened again and again since the end of the Second World War. Two million or so killed outright in Mao's Great Leap Forward in the 1950s (leaving aside the 20 to 30 million, perhaps as many as 45 million, who died of starvation), followed by another one to two million in the Cultural Revolution; half a million killed in Indonesia in 1965; another half million murdered by Idi Amin in Uganda, and two million by Pol Pot in Cambodia, in the 1970s; between fifty and a hundred thousand Kurds gassed by Saddam Hussein in the late 1980s; three quarters of a million Tutsis slaughtered by Hutus in the 1990s ... Genocide, attended by horrific cruelty, has been a regular pattern of post-World War II history, not something that ended with the death of Hitler. Refusing comparisons with the Holocaust keeps us from properly diagnosing the factors that can lead masses of people, peaceable and kind to their neighbors in general, to participate in or stand idly by crimes against humanity of this sort.

With that in mind, what are our responsibilities, as individuals, in the wake of the Holocaust? — in the light, more broadly, of a human history fraught with a tendency to engage in mass torture and murder? Of course I don't have anything remotely like a definitive answer to that question. I offer instead some tentative thoughts on the matter.

The political conditions that give rise to genocide have almost always consisted either of totalitarian dictatorship (Germany, China, Cambodia) or the breakdown of all political order (Indonesia, Rwanda, the former Yugoslavia). Those living in long-established liberal democracies have reason to suppose that such countries are not readily going to fall into either of these conditions. That said, sometimes the institutions even in these countries are so deeply threatened that the possibility of democratic collapse must be taken seriously.

But shoring up the institutions and procedures that make for stable liberal democracy is mostly a job *for* institutions themselves. Prosecutors and police forces and the military need to uphold the rule of law, rather than using their power to go after a would-be tyrant's enemies; legislators need to make laws that constrain the would-be tyrant; judges need to maintain their independence; journalists need to bring abuses to light, and fight back in court if their freedom is threatened. Many individual politicians and police officers and reporters will need to summon courage and doggedness to maintain checks on tyranny but the vast majority of a society's members do not occupy such positions and have little opportunity to preserve its institutions.

The question I want to take up, therefore, is what virtues we as individual citizens should cultivate, in our day-to-day interactions, in order to help keep our societies from sliding into tyranny and/or genocide. How should each of us act, and what attitudes should we have or display, even if we are not legislators or judges or police officers or journalists, to keep our country far from massive evil?

Well, one thing we need to do is try to ensure that we have the courage to stand up to an oppressive regime that demands that we conform to it. This is a crucial virtue. Certainly I would like to think that I would risk my life rather than tell an official how to find my Latino or Palestinian neighbor, if a campaign of massive expulsion or murder were to get underway in my country.

But the chances of anything quite this extreme happening are low in a stable democracy. And if it did happen, my individual resistance, were I brave enough to resist, would do little to stop the campaign. So the danger of cowardice in these extreme circumstances, important as it is, may not be what we most need to worry about.

Conformism is I think a greater danger. Cowardice and conformism are not the same thing. I may agree with what you say out of fear that you will hurt me or block my career, but I am at least as likely to agree out of a desire for your approval, or a sense that if you and others keep saying something ("Palestinians are terrorists"; "Latinos are a threat to our way of life"), then it must be true. No fear need come into my agreement. I may indeed not feel or think much at all; I may go along with you almost unconsciously.

But conformism is what leads prejudices to spread widely, lies told by public officials and propaganda outlets to go unchecked, uncomfortable truths to get dismissed or buried. Would-be tyrants thrive on the tendency of people to go along with what others say. That tendency can be surprisingly easily thwarted — studies have shown that even a single dissenter in a group can lead others to dissent as well. It is important therefore to cultivate a willingness to dissent from whatever form of "political correctness" dominates the circles in which we move.

To be clear, I don't mean by this that we should be contrarians, objecting to everything just for the sake of objecting, much less that we should listen to cranks rather than accepting mainstream scholarship and the mainstream media. Dissent for its own sake is pointless and a tendency to trust cranks is something that empowers charlatans and manipulators. No, our dissent needs to be responsible, based as much as possible on impartial information, and informed by an awareness of what impartial information looks like. To combat propaganda, we need a combination of independent and responsible thought. We need to avoid conforming, thoughtlessly, to the accepted wisdom around us, but we can only do that if we place a thoughtful trust in scholars and specialists who probe accepted wisdom and marshal evidence for the claims they make.

Independent and responsible thought is not enough, however, to forestall a slide towards totalitarianism. Two other post-Auschwitz virtues I would hold up are 1) a commitment to reform over resistance, and to nonviolent resistance, where needed, over violent resistance, and 2) a refusal to demonize anyone, even those who themselves demonize others.

Why favor reform over resistance, and insist on nonviolent resistance where reform seems impossible, or inadequate to the problems at hand? Would-be tyrants are not shy about using violence and are contemptuous of the procedural niceties by which reform, in liberal democracies, is supposed to be carried out. Why not fight fire with fire? Surely fighting fire with fire is the only appropriate response if an entire political system is corrupt. Then, there will be those who say, "The whole system must go." We must resist it altogether, they say, with violent means if necessary, rather than work within it — anything short of revolution is collaboration.

There is something appealing about this view, and I often feel naïve or cowardly when defending liberal caution to my more radical friends. But in countries that remain liberal democracies, even badly flawed ones, giving up on proceduralism and nonviolence is a grave mistake, both pragmatically and morally. Pragmatically, because the overthrow of a government by its people is very rare, and, where it proceeds through violence, it almost always leads to chaos and/or totalitarianism: the conditions for genocide. In 1985, the Marcoses were ousted from power by mass peaceful protests; in 1989, Communist governments fell across Europe in the same way. But the Tiananmen Square protests failed, the Arab Spring has had mostly disappointing outcomes, and violent revolutions across the centuries have almost always brought on harshly oppressive regimes in their wake. Reform movements that work through liberal procedures, by contrast, have often brought about real progress, if perhaps slower and less complete progress than their leaders had hoped for.

There are in addition deep moral problems with radicalism and violence. What am I telling my fellow citizens if I reject the entire system they live under — all the institutions by which they have hitherto run their lives — as unjust? That they are too stupid or self-deluded to see that themselves? That they do see it but are too lazy or too cowardly to do anything about it? That they *endorse* racism or sexism or classism? Any way you cut it, I display a breathtaking degree of contempt for their intelligence or moral qualities. I also display a great deal of arrogance. Do I think I am the only person, or one of a small handful, who can see through the lies or prejudices that blind everyone else? If I do think that, I am probably not the sort of person who should be leading a political or social movement. Arrogance of that sort bodes ill for what I and my allies will achieve, if we ever gain power.

Now there are peaceful ways of trying to upend a governmental system (think again of the Philippines in the 1980s, or East Germany). Even that, I think, should be a last resort; reform, working through a system rather than upending it, is normally preferable. But sometimes reform is not possible. In such cases, an entire people may break out in spontaneous demonstrations. And if that happens, I will not display contempt or arrogance by joining them.

But in acting *violently*, I am of necessity treating the objects of my violence without respect: I am saying that reasoning with them cannot bring about justice. So there is a deep contempt and arrogance built into any resort to violence. It may on occasion be necessary. I am not a pacifist, and would not rule out violence against oppressors where that is the only way to defeat them.

But protestors often turn to violence where it is clearly *not* the only way to combat oppression. In particular, it is fairly obvious that violence is not the only way to combat oppression where the rule of law remains intact, and where there is a free press and freedom of assembly. Here we should refrain wholly from violence: not just because of the physical harm it does, but because of the moral harm it does, to ourselves as well as to others. A refusal to engage in violence can by the same token be a moral discipline — a way of demonstrating humility, and inculcating it in ourselves. In the midst of political action even against great evils, we need to retain a respect for others, and a humility about our own insight and virtue.

This is a teaching we can learn from Gandhi. Nonviolent resistance, for him, was not merely a matter of refraining from killing and injuring others, nor did he justify it simply by pointing out that murder and injury are morally wrong. Instead, for Gandhi nonviolent resistance was an entire worldview, a set of attitudes by which one trusts that most of one's fellow human beings *want* justice and peace, and that if one acts in ways that show them respect, the path to justice and peace will become clear to them. I am not as optimistic as Gandhi was about either of these propositions, but I am convinced that we build a respectful society only by showing respect to one another. We will never defeat violence by becoming violent ourselves — we will simply give our opponents an excuse for their conduct, and make them look less bad to anyone wavering between them and us — and we can do a surprising amount of good by returning peace for war, respect for contempt, justice for injustice. It took a war to defeat the Nazis, but after that war was over, the Allies solidified their victory by helping Germans to build a liberal democracy for themselves. By contrast, the harsh punishments meted out to Germany after the first World War, meant to crush its imperial ambitions forever, led instead to the rise of Nazism, and a return of those ambitions in a more horrifying form than they had taken before. So the value of nonviolence, of showing people we oppose how to do things better rather than trying to crush them, is one message I would take away from Auschwitz.

For similar reasons, I think the final virtue we need to cultivate in ourselves is a refusal to demonize others — even the people who themselves demonize various groups. What is "demonization"? To answer that question, it's helpful to take the "demon" in demonization seriously. A demon is an unalterably evil being, radically unlike human beings in its desire for evil for its own sake and its imperviousness to repentance. A demon is utterly unlike us; we cannot empathize with it. We therefore need not try to explain its behavior in terms of human tendencies we ourselves might share; we can crush it without mercy; and we can congratulate ourselves on not being remotely like it.

Seeing people this way has a whole array of dangerous consequences. Most obviously, when we demonize people, we give ourselves an excuse for subjecting them to any and every kind of ill treatment. A demon is absolutely evil: beyond rehabilitation and without any value that deserves respect or preservation. A demon is not really human, so the norms of shared humanity do not apply to him; even the concern we have for animals does not apply to him. On the contrary, in the name of all we value, including the members of "real" humanity, we need to do whatever we can to protect ourselves against him. So in regarding people as demons, we lift all moral barriers against treating them inhumanely. If we are wrong, then we have licensed ourselves to commit the greatest of evils: to become ourselves as close as human beings can to being demons.

In addition, by demonizing another, we relieve ourselves of the responsibility to figure out what explicable, and potentially remediable, causes may have led to such behavior. Possibly there is a neurological condition that can be cured or a childhood trauma is involved and there are ways that can be controlled. Possibly extreme poverty, or the brutality and injustice of others, have led the individual to commit terrible acts. Discovering causes like these for such dispositions may mean we can help the individual overcome those dispositions, and even if beyond help, such a diagnosis may enable us to prevent others from developing similar dispositions. By demonizing others, we cut ourselves off from these humane responses to evil.

We also cut ourselves off from examining our own conduct, and seeing how we may have contributed to the evil of others. Demonization is most likely to occur in conflict situations — between groups or individuals embroiled in a feud. Engaging in it relieves each side of considering their own responsibility for that conflict. Of course, responsibility for a conflict does not always belong equally to both sides, and we may rightly see our opponents as having committed grave moral wrongs. But by demonizing them, we remove the need even to consider whether we have harmed them. That is conducive to arrogant self-congratulation on our part. We are unlikely in any case to take steps that might alleviate the conflict between us.

Now the moral dangers of demonization also constitute its temptations. We *want* to clear ourselves of all responsibility in a conflict. We *want* to see ourselves, and present ourselves to others, as upright innocents, against whom our enemies have perpetrated unwarranted aggression. And we want to see our enemies as objects, who can be dealt with as we see fit. To take responsibility for wrongdoings on our own part means we may have to compromise interests we hold dear, and will in any case have to change some of what we have been doing. Treating our enemies as demons instead is thus convenient as well as psychologically comforting. Both the convenience and the comfort are however temptations to evil. By demonizing others, we cut ourselves off from seeing our responsibility for our relationship to them and close off our ability to relate to them under the rubric of shared humanity. That is always a grave wrong. We need instead to see every evildoer, even a Hitler or a Charles Manson, as someone we ourselves could be, if we lived in other circumstances. Only a commitment to seeing myself in every other human being enables me to work together with all humanity in the effort to prevent and heal evil, in others as well as in myself.

Which brings us back to the reason why we must be willing to make comparisons between the Holocaust and other events. We must compare Hitler's atrocities with other genocides, and the conditions that brought Hitler to power with conditions we may see around us, because we need to recognize the tendencies to inhumanity and complicity and cowardice in ourselves that might lead us to become, or to support, a racist tyrant. Only then do we have any hope of wrestling with these tendencies, and disabling them. Of course, we should be careful to note differences between the Nazis and ourselves as well. The key is to acknowledge our capacity to succumb to evil; to assume otherwise is both foolish and disingenuous. It blocks us from seeing our own tendencies to inhumanity. Indeed, it may even blind us, like the "ordinary Germans" who kept their head down in the 1930s, to gross inhumanity being done currently in our name.

So:

1    courage

2    independent thought, fending off conformism

3    responsible thought, fending off cranks

4    nonviolence

and

5    a refusal to demonize anyone, even those who themselves demonize people

Would the widespread cultivation of these virtues end genocide and tyranny? I don't know. But it would surely help. And it would in any case be a fine way for us to honor the victims who died at Auschwitz: to stand up, in their name, for the humanity that was denied to them.

# Contributors

## FOREWORD: Confronting the Past, for the Sake of the Future

**Anna Ornstein** – Anna Ornstein is Professor Emerita of Child Psychiatry, University of Cincinnati, Former Co-Director, International Center for the Study of Psychoanalytic Self-Psychology, Lecturer in Psychiatry, Harvard Medical School, Training and Supervising Analyst at the Cincinnati Psychoanalytic Institute, Supervising Analyst at the Boston Psychoanalytic Society and Institute (BPSI) and Massachusetts Institute for Psychoanalysis; instrumental in developing and leading the self-psychology movement, she has authored over 100 publications that cover a wide range of topics, including the interpretive process in psychoanalysis, psychoanalytic psychotherapy, child psycho-therapy, treatment of children and families, and the process of recovery following survival of extreme conditions; she earned her medical degree from Heidelberg University School of Medicine, and is a graduate of the Chicago Institute for Psychoanalysis; she has been the recipient of numerous awards related to both her work in medicine and in Holocaust education including the American Psychiatric Association's Distinguished Psychiatrist Lecturer Award (1989), Rosenberry Award for Dedication to the care of children (1991), University of Cincinnati Award for Excellence in Research and Scholarship (1996), American Psychiatric Association's Special Presidential Commendation (2000), Boston Psychoanalytic Society and Institute's Arthur R. Kravitz Award for Community Action and Humanitarian Contributions "in recognition of a lifetime of dedication to teaching about the Holocaust" (2018); In 2004 she published her memoir, *My Mother's Eyes: Holocaust Memories of a Young Girl*, a collection of short stories of her life during the war.

**Joy Ladin** – Joy Ladin is the author of eleven books including most recently, the revised second edition of *The Book of Anna* (EOAGH) winner, 2021 National Jewish Book Award for Poetry; her works include Forward Fives Award winners, and Lambda and Triangle Award finalists; she is a recipient of a National Endowment for the Arts writing fellowship and two Hadassah Brandeis Institute Research fellowships; she is a recipient of the Keshet Hachamat Lev award, has hosted a weekly conversation program "Containing Multitudes," is a TEDx presenter, and has been featured on Krista Tippett's "On Being" NPR broadcast; she has held the David and Ruth Gottesman Chair in English at Stern College of Yeshiva University; her scholarly work has been supported by a Fulbright Scholarship and an American Council of Learned

Societies Research Fellowship; she holds a Ph.D. in American Literature from Princeton University, there awarded the Porter Ogden Jacobus Fellowship as top graduate student in the Humanities, an M.F.A. in Creative Writing from the University of Massachusetts (Amherst), and a B.A. from Sarah Lawrence College.

## PART I: The Rise of Nazism and Heightening Antisemitism

**Yehoshua November** – Yehoshua November is the author of two poetry collections, *God's Optimism* (a finalist for the *Los Angeles Times* Book Prize) and *Two Worlds Exist* (a finalist for the National Jewish Book Award and the Paterson Poetry Prize). His work has been featured in *The New York Times Magazine, Harvard Divinity Bulletin, The Sun, Prairie Schooner, Tikkun, Virginia Quarterly Review,* and on National Public Radio and On Being's Poetry Unbound podcast program.

**Jane Yolen** – Jane Yolen has published 376 books, from board books, picture books, children's poetry books, YA novels, short stories, cook books, music books, adult novels, short story collections, poetry, anthologies. Her books and stories have won the Jewish Book Award, Nebulas, World Fantasy Awards, Caldecott; recipient of 6 honorary doctorates, she has also taught children's literature at Smith College and was the first woman to give the Andrew Lang lecture, a lecture series which dates to 1927, at St Andrews University in Scotland.

**Julia Kolchinsky Dasbach** – Julia Kolchinsky Dasbach came to the United States as a Jewish refugee in 1993, from Dnipro, Ukraine, and grew up in the DC metro area suburb of Rockville, Maryland. She earned a Ph.D in Comparative Literature and Literary Theory from the University of Pennsylvania for her dissertation, *Lyric Witness: Intergenerational (Re)collection of the Holocaust in Contemporary American Poetry;* her newest collection is *40 Weeks* (YesYes Books). She is also the author of *The Many Names for Mother*, selected by Ellen Bass as the winner of the 2018 Stan and Tom Wick Poetry prize and finalist for the Jewish Book Award. Her second collection, *Don't Touch the Bones* (Lost Horse Press) won the 2019 Idaho Poetry Prize. Her poetry appears in *POETRY, American Poetry Review*, and *The Nation*, among others.

**Tony Barnstone** – Tony Barnstone teaches at Whittier College and is the author of 22 books, a music CD, and a creativity tool: The Radiant Tarot: Pathway to Creativity. His poetry books include *Pulp Sonnets; Beast in the Apartment; Tongue of War: From Pearl Harbor to Nagasaki; The Golem of Los Angeles; Sad Jazz; and Impure*. He is also a co-translator of Chinese literature, anthologist, and world literature textbook editor. Among his awards: The Poets Prize, Grand Prize of the Strokestown International Poetry Contest, Pushcart Prize, John Ciardi Prize, Benjamin Saltman Award, and fellowships from the NEA, the NEH, and the California Arts Council.

**Dan Bellm** – Dan Bellm is the author of four books of poetry, including *Deep Well* (Lavender Ink, 2017) and *Practice: A Book of Midrash* (Sixteen Rivers, 2008), which won the 2009 California Book Award. Books of poetry in translation include *Speaking in Song*, by Mexican poet Pura López Colomé (Shearsman, UK, 2017) *and The Song of the Dead*, by French poet Pierre Reverdy (Black Square, 2016). He lives in Berkeley, California, and teaches literary translation and poetry at Antioch University Los Angeles. www.danbellm.com.

**Steven Sher** – Brooklyn-born Steven Sher has lived in Jerusalem since 2012. He is the author of 19 books (poetry and prose). His recent titles are *Contestable Truths, Incontestable Lies* (Dos Madres Press, 2019), chronicling the challenges to survival in contemporary Israel; *What Comes from the Heart: Poems in the Jewish Tradition* (Cyberwit, 2020); and the forthcoming *When They Forget* (New Feral Press), a selection of his poems about the Shoah. His writing on the subject has appeared widely, including as contributor to *Blood to Remember: American Poets on the Holocaust*. A 2018 recipient of the Glenna Luschei Distinguished Poet Award, he continues to teach (workshops/ visiting writer) in the U.S. and Israel after having taught at many U.S. universities and having worked as an editor/consultant across the print media/publishing/literary spectrum since the 1970s.

**Mark Budman** – Mark Budman was born in the former Soviet Union, and English is a second language for him. His fiction and non-fiction writing has appeared or is forthcoming in such publications as *Witness, Catapult, American Scholar, Guernica/PEN, Huffington Post, World Literature Today, Daily Science Fiction, Mississippi Review, Virginia Quarterly, The London Magazine (UK), McSweeney's, Sonora Review, Another Chicago, Sou'wester, Southeast Review, Mid-American Review, Painted Bride Quarterly, the W.W. Norton anthology Flash Fiction Forward, Not Quite What I Was Planning: Six-Word Memoirs by Writers Famous and Obscure, Short Fiction (UK)*, and elsewhere. He was the publisher of the flash fiction magazine *Vestal Review* between 2000 and 2020. His novel *My Life at First Try* was published by Counterpoint Press.

**Robert Perry Ivey** – Robert Perry Ivey, born in Forsyth, GA, grew up in Macon and is a Lecturer at Gordon State College and was the Visiting McEver Chair of Poetry at the Georgia Institute of Technology (Georgia Tech) from 2012-2013. Ivey earned an M.A. in English Literature from Georgia State University and a M.F.A from Sarah Lawrence College in Creative Writing. He is the author of the chapbooks *Southbound* and *Letters to My Daughter*, recipient of The Academy of American Poetry's John B. Santoianni Award, and his work has appeared in numerous literary journals and in several anthologies. Ivey also co-wrote a short film, *The Long Con Mom*, which won Best Cinematography at the 2018 Marietta Film Festival in Atlanta, Georgia.

**Peter Serchuk** – Peter Serchuk's poems have appeared in numerous literary journals including the *Hudson Review, Poetry, American Poetry Review, Boulevard, Denver Quarterly, Texas Review, Atlanta Review, New Letters, Valparaiso Poetry Review* and others. He is the author of *Waiting for Poppa at the Smithtown Diner* (University of Illinois Press), *All That Remains* (WordTech Editions) and *The Purpose of Things* (Regal House Publishing). He lives in Carmel, CA. More at peterserchuk.com.

**Geoffrey Philp** – Born in Jamaica, Geoffrey Philp is the author of the novel, *Garvey's Ghost*. His work is represented in nearly every major anthology of Caribbean literature, including the *Oxford Book of Caribbean Short Stories* and *Oxford Book of Caribbean Verse*. He has published eight books of poetry including most recently *Archipelagos* (Peepal Tree Press, 2023). He has also published two books of short stories, *Uncle Obadiah and the Alien* and *Who's Your Daddy*. *Benjamin, My Son*, his first novel, was nominated for the IMPAC Dublin Literary Prize. Through DNA testing, he recently discovered his Sephardic Jewish ancestry and is currently working on a book of poems about the Holocaust. Philp's work is featured on The Poetry Rail at The Betsy in a homage to 12 writers that shaped Miami culture.

**Nancy Naomi Carlson** – Nancy Naomi Carlson, winner of the 2022 Oxford-Weidenfeld Translation Prize, is a poet, translator, essayist, and editor, as well as a recipient of two literature translation fellowships from the National Endowment for the Arts. She has also received grants from the Maryland State Arts Council and the Albertine Translation Fund (2023). Author of four non-translated titles and eight books of translations, her full-length collection of poems, *An Infusion of Violets* (Seagull Books), published in 2019 was featured in *The New York Times Book Review* ("New & Noteworthy"), Her third full-length poetry collection, *Piano in the Dark,* is forthcoming from Seagull Books. www.nancynaomicarlson.com

**Alejandro Escude** – Alejandro Escudé's first book of poems, *My Earthbound Eye*, was published in September 2013 upon winning the 2012 Sacramento Poetry Center Award. He received a master's degree in creative writing from UC Davis, where he was taught by such notable poets as Gary Snyder and Sandra McPherson. Alejandro works as an English teacher, having taught in a variety of school systems at the secondary level for over fifteen years. Originally from Córdoba, Argentina, he immigrated to California many years ago at the age of six. A new collection, *The Book of the Unclaimed Dead*, published by Main Street Rag Press, is now available at mainstreetrag.com. Alejandro is a single dad of two wonderful kids and lives in Los Angeles with his dog, a terrier named Jake.

**Su Hwang** – Su Hwang is the author of *Bodega*, published by Milkweed Editions, which received the 2020 Minnesota Book Award in poetry and was named a finalist for the 2021 Kate Tufts Discovery Award. She is the recipient of the inaugural Jerome Hill Fellowship in Literature, the Academy of America Poets James Wright Prize, and writer-in-residence fellowships to Dickinson House and Hedgebrook, among others. Born in Seoul, Korea, she has called NYC and San Francisco home before transplanting to the Twin Cities in 2013 to attend the University of Minnesota, where she received her MFA in poetry. She is a teaching artist and Outreach Manager with the Minnesota Prison Writing Workshop (MPWW), and is the co-founder of *Poetry Asylum*.

**Philip Terman** – Philip Terman is the author of six collections of poems including, *This Crazy Devotion* (Broadstone Books, 2020). His poems have appeared in numerous journals and anthologies, including *Poetry*, *The Georgia Review*, *The Kenyon Review*, *The Sun Magazine*, *The Forward*, *The Autumn House Anthology of Contemporary Poetry*, *The New Promised Land: An Anthology of Jewish American Poetry* and *99 Poems for the 99 Percent*. A collection of his poems, *My Dear Friend Kafka*, has been translated into Arabic. He's a retired professor of English at Clarion University and founded The Bridge Literary Arts Center in Franklin, PA. He has collaborated with other artists, including composers, painters, and sculptors, and several of his poems have been set to orchestra and the song cycles: *The Gatherer of Lost Children, The Four Seasons,* and *The Silence Flowering Its Birdsong,* by the composer Brent Register. www.philipterman.com.

**Gretchen Primack** – Gretchen Primack is the author of *Visiting Days* (Willow Books 2019), set in a maximum-security men's prison, as well as two other poetry collections: *Kind* (Post-Traumatic Press), which explores the dynamic between humans and (other) animals, and *Doris' Red Spaces* (Mayapple Press). She also co-wrote, with Jenny Brown, *The Lucky Ones: My Passionate Fight for Farm Animals* (Penguin Avery). Her poems have appeared in *The Paris Review, Prairie Schooner, FIELD, Ploughshares, Poet Lore,* and other journals. Primack has administrated and taught with college programs in prison for many years, and she moonlights at an indie bookstore in Woodstock, NY.

**Sue William Silverman** – Sue William Silverman is the author of four memoirs: *How to Survive Death and Other Inconveniences*, the University of Nebraska Press, American Lives Series; *The Pat Boone Fan Club: My Life as a White Anglo-Saxon Jew*, the University of Nebraska Press, American Lives Series; *Because I Remember Terror, Father, I Remember You*, winner of the Association of Writers and Writing Programs Award Series in Creative Nonfiction. Her memoir *Love Sick: One Woman's Journey through Sexual Addiction* was also made into a Lifetime TV Original Movie. Her craft book is *Fearless Confessions: A Writer's Guide to Memoir*, and her poetry collections are *If the Girl Never Learns* and *Hieroglyphics in Neon*. She teaches in the MFA Writing Program at Vermont College of Fine Arts. www.SueWilliamSilverman.com.

## PART I ESSAY: The Times and the Holocaust (an historical and geopolitical perspective)

**C. Paul Vincent** – Paul Vincent is the Keene State College Professor Emeritus of Holocaust Studies and History. He founded and then chaired the Department of Holocaust and Genocide Studies during 2009-2017 and served as Director of the Cohen Center for Holocaust Studies from 1998 to 2007. He was the Pinchas and Mark Wisen Fellow at the Center for Advanced Holocaust Studies, the United States Holocaust Memorial Museum (2007–08), and a Fulbright Scholar and then Visiting Professor at Jagiellonian University, Krakow, Poland (2015 and 2018). His published work includes *The Politics of Hunger: The Blockade of Germany, 1915–1919* (Ohio University Press, 1985), *A Historical Dictionary of Germany's Weimar Republic, 1918–1933* (Greenwood Press, 1997), and "The Voyage of the St. Louis Revisited" (Holocaust and Genocide Studies, Fall 2011). He holds a BS in Political Science, Oregon State University; MA in History, University of Northern Colorado; MA in Library Science, University of Michigan; and PhD in History, University of Colorado.

## PART II: Forced Labor, Ghettos, Extermination

**Ben Banyard** – Ben Banyard is a UK-based poet who grew up in Birmingham, but now lives in Portishead on the Severn Estuary with his wife and two young children. He's published a pamphlet, *Communing* (Indigo Dreams, 2016) and two full collections, *We Are All Lucky* (Indigo Dreams, 2018) and *Hi-Viz* (Yaffle Press, 2021). He blogs at https://benbanyard.wordpress.com

**Judith Baumel** – Judith Baumel's books are *The Weight of Numbers*, for which she won The Walt Whitman Award of the Academy of American Poets; *Now*; *The Kangaroo Girl*; *Passeggiate* and *Thorny*. She is Professor Emerita of English and Founding Director of the Creative Writing Program at Adelphi University. She has served as President of The Association of Writers and Writing Programs, director of The Poetry Society of America and as a Fulbright Scholar in Italy.

**Marge Piercy** – Marge Piercy has written 17 novels including The New York Times Bestseller *Gone To Soldiers*; the National Bestsellers *Braided Lives* and *The Longings of Women*; the classics *Woman on the Edge of Time* and *He, She and It*; and *Sex Wars*. Her 20 volumes of poetry include *On the Way Out, Turn Off the Light*. Her critically acclaimed memoir is *Sleeping with Cats*. Born in center city Detroit, educated at the University of Michigan and Northwestern, the recipient of four honorary doctorates, she is active in antiwar, feminist and environmental causes. She has read, given workshops or speeches in over 500 venues in the U.S. and abroad, including residences at several synagogues. Her work has been translated into 22 languages. She has written liturgy used in Reconstructionist and Reform prayer books and services.

**Ellen Bass** – Ellen Bass's collection, *Indigo,* was published by Copper Canyon Press in 2020. Her other poetry books include *Like a Beggar, The Human Line,* and *Mules of Love*. Her poems appear frequently in *The New Yorker, American Poetry Review,* and many other journals. Among her awards are Fellowships from the Guggenheim Foundation, The NEA, and The California Arts Council, The Lambda Literary Award, and four Pushcart Prizes. She co-edited the first major anthology of women's poetry, *No More Masks!*, and her nonfiction books include the groundbreaking *The Courage to Heal: A Guide for Women Survivors of Child Sexual Abuse* and *Free Your Mind: The Book for Gay, Lesbian and Bisexual Youth*. A Chancellor Emerita of the Academy of American Poets, Bass founded poetry workshops at Salinas Valley State Prison and the Santa Cruz, California jails, and teaches in the MFA writing program at Pacific University.

**Greg Harris** – Greg Harris has taught writing at Harvard University since 2003. Founding editor of *Pangyrus LitMag*, Greg has been recipient of a Fulbright Fellowship and grants from the National Endowment for the Humanities and Oregon's Regional Arts and Culture Council. His audio recording "Champion of Hot Peppers" won a 2001 NAPPA Gold Medal for storytelling. His translation of Seno Gumira Ajidarma's novel *Jazz, Perfume, and the Incident* was published as part of the Modern Library of Indonesia (2012). His essays, reviews, and stories have appeared or are forthcoming in the *Washington Post, Boston Globe,* the *Chronicle of Higher Education, Harvard Review, Earth Island Journal,* and elsewhere. He is currently shopping a novel about the survival of the Bulgarian Jews in World War II.

**Raficq Abdulla** – Raficq Abdulla (1940-2019) a South African-born lawyer, writer, public speaker and broadcaster was Visiting Fellow of the Faculty of Business and Law, Kingston University. He was also a founder member of the Advisory Panel of the Muslim Law Shariah Council (UK) and a trustee of the Poetry Society, Planet Poetry and of PEN. In 1999, he was awarded an MBE for his interfaith work among Muslims, Jews, and Christians. His literary works include poetry based on the Muslim mystics Rumi and Attar, *Words of Paradise and Conference of the Birds*, and reflections on the sonnets of Shakespeare, *Reflecting Mercury: Dreaming Shakespeare's Sonnets*. He is co-author of *Understanding Sharia – Islamic Law in a Globalised World* (I.B. Tauris, 2018).

**Jacqueline Osherow** – Jacqueline Osherow is the author of nine collections of poetry, including *Divine Ratios* (LSU Press, 2023.) She's received grants from the John Simon Guggenheim Foundation, the National Endowment for the Arts, the Ingram Merrill Foundation and the Witter Bynner Prize from the American Academy and Institute of Arts and Letters, as well as a number of prizes from the Poetry Society of America. Her poems have appeared in many magazines, journals and anthologies, *including The New Yorker, The Paris Review, American Poetry Review, the Norton Anthology of Jewish-American Literature, Wadsworth Anthology of Poetry, Best American Poetry 2018*. She's Distinguished Professor of English at the University of Utah.

**Bruce Black** – Bruce Black is the author of *Writing Yoga* (Rodmell Press/ Shambhala) and editorial director of The Jewish Writing Project. He received his BA from Columbia University and his MFA from Vermont College. His work has appeared in *Elephant Journal, Blue Lyra Review, Tiferet Journal, Hevria, Poetica, Reform Judaism, The Jewish Literary Journal, Mindbodygreen, Yogi Times, Chicken Soup for the Soul*, and elsewhere. He lives in Sarasota, FL.

**Erin Redfern** – Erin Redfern is the author of *Spellbreaking and Other Life Skills* (Blue Lyra Press Delphi Series, 2016) and 2016 co-recipient of the Poetry Society of America's Robert H Winner Award. Her work appears among others in the *New Ohio Review, Massachusetts Review*, and *North American Review*, where it was runner-up for the 2020 James Hearst Prize. She earned her PhD at Northwestern University, where she was also a Fellow at the Searle Center for Teaching Excellence. As sources for her work in *New Voices* she would like to acknowledge the US Holocaust Memorial Museum's online exhibit of the Hoecker album; Rachel Century, whose dissertation on female administrators of the Third Reich is available online through the University of London; and Ada Ushpiz's documentary "Vita Activa: the Spirit of Hannah Arendt."

**Andrew McFadyen-Ketchum** – Andrew McFadyen-Ketchum is an author, editor, & ghostwriter. He is author of three poetry collections, *Fight or Flight, Visiting Hours* and *Ghost Gear*; Editor of *Apocalypse Now: Poems & Prose from the End of Days*; Acquisitions Editor for Upper Rubber Boot Books; Founder and Editor of PoemoftheWeek.com and The Floodgate Poetry Series; Learn more at AndrewMK.com

**Susanna Lang** – Susanna Lang's third collection of poems, *Travel Notes from the River Styx*, was released in 2017 from Terrapin Books. Her previous collection was *Tracing the Lines* (Brick Road Poetry Press, 2013). A two-time Hambidge fellow, her poems have appeared in such publications as *Little Star, Prairie Schooner, December, American Life in Poetry* and *Verse Daily*. Her translations of poetry by Yves Bonnefoy include *Words in Stone* and *The Origin of Language*. She lives and teaches in Chicago. More at www.susannalang.com.

**Bruce Bond** – Bruce Bond is the author of twenty-eight books including, most recently, *Blackout Starlight: New and Selected Poems 1997-2015* (E. Phillabaum Award, LSU, 2017), *Rise and Fall of the Lesser Sun Gods* (Elixir Prize, Elixir Press, 2018), *Frankenstein's Children* (Lost Horse, 2018), *Dear Reader* (Parlor, 2018), *Plurality and the Poetics of Self* (Palgrave, 2019), *Words Written Against the Walls of the City* (LSU, 2019), *Scar* (Etruscan, 2020), *Behemoth* (New Criterion Prize, Criterion Books), *The Calling* (Parlor, 2021), *Patmos* (Juniper Prize, UMass, 2021), *Liberation of Dissonance* (Nicholas Schaffner Award for Literature in Music, Schaffner Press, 2022), *Choreomania* (MadHat, 2022), and *Invention of the Wilderness* (LSU, 2022). His work has appeared in numerous journals and anthologies, including seven editions of *Best American Poetry*. Presently he is Regents Emeritus Professor of English at the University of North Texas.

**Alan Catlin** – Alan Catlin has been publishing steadily since the 70's. His credits include some of the most obscure, and some of the most revered, literary venues for poetry: *Wordsworth's Socks, Wormwood Review, Descant*, and *The Literary Review*. He has published dozens of chapbooks and full-length books, including more recently *Asylum Garden: after Van Gogh* (Dos Madres Press), *Lessons in Darkness* (Luchador Press a division of Spartan Books), *The Blue Hotel*, (Cyberwit), *Memories* (Alien Buddha Press). and *Memories Too* (Dos Madres Press) He is the poetry editor of the online poetry and review journal, *Misfit magazine*.

**Sara Lippmann** – Sara Lippmann is the author of the story collections *Doll Palace*, re-released by 713 Books, and *Jerks* from Mason Jar Press. Her work has been honored by the New York Foundation for the Arts, and has appeared in *The Millions, The Washington Post, The Lit Hub, Best Small Fictions, Catapult, Guernica, Epiphany, Split Lip, Joyland, Wigleaf* and elsewhere. She received a BA from Brown and an MFA from The New School, Currently, she teaches with Jericho Writers. For many years, she co-hosted the Sunday Salon, a longstanding NYC reading series Her debut novel, *LECH*, is out now from Tortoise Books. Find her @saralippmann or saralippmann.com

**Marilyn Kallet** – Marilyn Kallet has published 18 books, including *How Our Bodies Learned*, 2018, *The Love That Moves Me* and *Packing Light: New and Selected Poems*, Black Widow Press. She translated Paul Eluard's *Last Love Poems* and Péret's *The Big Game*. Dr. Kallet served as Knoxville Poet Laureate and is Professor Emerita at the University of Tennessee. She leads poetry residencies in Auvillar, for VCCA-France. She has performed her work on campuses across the U.S. and in France and Poland, as a guest of the U.S. Embassy's "America Presents" program. "American Diversity Report" hosted her dialogue with Maria James-Thiaw on "Black-Jewish Podcast: Poets Speak."

## PART II ESSAY: Humanity's Inhumanity
## (a sociological perspective)

**Rob Rosenthal** – Rob Rosenthal is John E. Andrus Professor of Sociology, emeritus, at Wesleyan University, and occasionally its Provost, he grew up outside New York. He graduated from Livingston College, and received an MA and PhD in Sociology from UC Santa Barbara. Among his works are *Homeless in Paradise*, *Playing for Change*, and *Pete Seeger in His Own Words*.

## PART III: Escape, Rescue, Resistance

**Tim Seibles** – Tim Seibles, a Philadelphia Native, is the author of a number of books of poetry including *Fast Animal* a finalist for the 2012 National Book Award and winner of the triennial Theodore Roethke Memorial Poetry Prize in 2013, and *One Turn Around The Sun* which was released in 2017. He has been Poet Laureate of Virginia and was professor of English and Creative Writing at Old Dominion University in Norfolk, Virginia.

**Ami Kaye** – Ami Kaye is the publisher of Glass Lyre Press, and founding editor of Pirene's Fountain and the Aeolian Harp Series. She has guided numerous books, chapbooks, and anthologies to print. Her poems, reviews, and articles have appeared in various publications, and received nominations for the Pushcart and James B. Baker Prizes. Ami published the benefit anthologies: *Sunrise from Blue Thunder* (for the Japan 2011 disasters), *Carrying the Branch: Poets in Search of Peace*, and *Collateral Damage* for disadvantaged children. She is the author of *What Hands Can Hold*.

**Jonathan Kinsman** – Jonathan Kinsman (he/him) is a trans poet from Manchester. Raised Church of England and with a background in theological study he lives his life marrying his spirituality and their sexuality. As well as being founding editor of Riggwelter press and associate editor of *Three Drops from a Cauldron*, he is also a BBC Edinburgh fringe slam finalist. He received a distinction for his MA in creative writing at the University of Sheffield. His debut pamphlet *&* was joint winner of the Indigo Dreams Pamphlet Prize in 2017 and his second, *Witness*, was published by Burning Eye in 2020.

**Cheryl J. Fish** – Cheryl J. Fish is an environmental justice scholar, fiction writer and poet. Her short stories have appeared in *Iron Horse Literary Review*, *From Somewhere to Nowhere: The End of the American Dream,* (Autonomedia Press, 2017), among others. Her books of poetry include *Crater & Tower* and *The Sauna is Full of Maids*. Her poems have appeared in journals and anthologies, including *Poetics-for-the-More-than-Human-World*, *New American Writing*, *Newtown Literary*, *Terrain.org*, *Reed*, and *Hanging Loose*. Her short fiction has been published in *Iron Horse Literary Review*, *CheapPop*, *Spank the Carp*, and *Liar's League*. *Off the Yoga Mat*, her debut novel was published by Livingston Press (2022). Fish has been Fulbright professor in Finland, writer-in-residence at Mount St. Helens National Volcanic Monument, and she is professor of English at Borough of Manhattan Community College, City University of New York.

**Cyril Wong** – Cyril Wong is a two-time Singapore Literature Prize-winning poet and the recipient of the Singapore National Arts Council's Young Artist Award for Literature. His books include poetry collections *Tilting Our Plates to Catch the Light* (2007) and *The Lover's Inventory* (2015), novels *The Last Lesson of Mrs de Souza* (2013) and *This Side of Heaven* (2020), and fiction collection *Ten Things My Father Never Taught Me* (2014). He completed his doctoral degree in English Literature at the National University of Singapore in 2012. His works have been featured in the Norton anthology, *Language for a New Century*, in *Chinese Erotic Poems* by Everyman's Library, and in magazines and journals around the world. His writings have been translated into Turkish, German, Italian, French, Portuguese and Japanese.

**Dina Elenbogen** – Dina Elenbogen, a widely published and award-winning poet and prose writer, is author of the memoir, *Drawn from Water: an American Poet, an Ethiopian Family, an Israeli Story* (BkMKPress, University of Missouri) and the poetry collection, *Apples of the Earth* (Spuyten Duvil, New York.) She has received fellowships from the Illinois Arts Council and the Ragdale Foundation and her work has appeared in anthologies including *Lost on the Map of the World* (Peter Lang, NY), *Where We Find Ourselves* (SUNY,NY), *Beyond Lament* (Northwestern University Press) *Rust Belt Chicago* and magazines including *Lit Hub, Bellevue Literary Review, Prairie Schooner, Poet Lore, December, Woven Tale Press, Times of Israel*, etc. She has a poetry MFA from the Iowa Writer's Workshop and teaches creative writing at the University of Chicago Graham School.

**Lauren Camp** – Lauren Camp is the author of five books, most recently *Took House* (Tupelo Press), and the forthcoming An Eye in Each Square (River River Books). Honors include the Dorset Prize, the Anna Davidson Rosenberg Award, and finalist citations for the Arab American Book Award, North American Book Award, and New Mexico-Arizona Book Award. Her poems have appeared in *Witness, Poet Lore, Kenyon Review, and World Literature Today,* and her work has been translated into Mandarin, Turkish, Spanish, Serbian and Arabic. An emeritus fellow of the Black Earth Institute, she lives and teaches in New Mexico. www.laurencamp.com

**Wendy Brandmark** – Wendy Brandmark is a novelist and short story writer. She won the Bridport Short Story Prize and has published stories widely in journals, including *North American Review, The Massachusetts Review, Stand Magazine* and *Lilith Magazine*. Her short story collection, *He Runs the Moon: Tales from the Cities*, was longlisted for Edgehill Prize. Her novel, *The Stray American*, was shortlisted for the Jerwood Fiction Uncovered Prize. She explored racism and difference in her novel, *The Angry Gods*. She has reviewed fiction for *The Times Literary Supplement, The Literary Review* and *The Independent*. She supervises students in fiction writing in the MST in Creative Writing at Oxford University.

**Becky Tuch** – Becky Tuch is a fiction and nonfiction writer based in Philadelphia, PA. She has been honored with awards and fellowships from The MacDowell Colony, The Somerville, MA Arts Council, *Moment Magazine*, *Glimmer Train*, and elsewhere. Her short fiction has appeared in numerous magazines and anthologies including *Gulf Coast, Post Road, Salt Hill, Tikkun Magazine* and *Best of the Net*. She is the Founding Editor of *The Review Review*, and now writes *The Lit Mag News Roundup*, a newsletter dedicated to lit mag publishing. Find her at BeckyTuch.com.

**TC Tolbert** – TC Tolbert identifies as a trans and genderqueer feminist, collaborator, maker, and poet. And, s/he's a human in love with humans doing human things. S/he is author of *Gephyromania* (Ahsahta Press 2014 and re-released in 2022 by Nightboat Books), five chapbooks, and co-editor of *Troubling the Line: Trans and Genderqueer Poetry and Poetics* (Nightboat Books 2013). TC was awarded an Academy of American Poets' Laureate Fellowship in 2019 for his work with trans, non-binary, and queer folks as Tucson's Poet Laureate. S/he also loves collaborating with wood. www.tctolbert.com

**Cortney Lamar Charleston** – Cortney Lamar Charleston's poems have appeared in a range of publications, including *POETRY, The Nation, The Atlantic, The American Poetry Review* and *Granta*. A Pushcart Prize-winning poet, Charleston has received a Ruth Lilly and Dorothy Sargent Rosenberg Fellowship from the Poetry Foundation as well as fellowships from Cave Canem, The Conversation Literary Festival and the New Jersey State Council on the Arts. His debut full-length poetry collection, Telepathologies, was selected by D.A. Powell for the 2016 Saturnalia Books Poetry Prize and released in 2017. His second full-length collection, *Doppelgangbanger*, was released in 2021 by Haymarket Books.

**Fabienne Josaphat** – Fabienne Josaphat is the author of *Dancing in the Baron's Shadow*, a debut novel released with Unnamed Press and translated into French by Calmann-Levy. Her essay, "Summer is an Empty House" made the Notable Essays mentions *in Best American Essays* 2016. Her fiction, non-fiction and poetry have been featured in *The Master's Review, Grist Journal, Damselfly, Hinchas de Poesia, Off the Coast Journal* and *The Caribbean Writer*, as well as in *Eight Miami Poets*, a Jai-Alai Books poetry anthology. She lives in South Florida.

**Lois P. Jones** – Lois P. Jones was a finalist for the 2022 Best Spiritual Literature Award in Poetry from Orison Books. Her work was Highly Commended and published in the 2021 Bridport Poetry Prize Anthology and twice longlisted for the National Poetry Competition. Other honors include the Bristol Poetry Prize judged by Liz Berry, the Lascaux Poetry Prize for a single poem, the Tiferet Poetry Prize and winning finalist for the 2018 Terrain Poetry contest judged by Jane Hirshfield. Jones has work published or forthcoming in the *Academy of American Poets* – *Poem A Day, Poetry Wales, Plume, Guernica Editions, Verse Daily, Tupelo Quarterly, Tinderbox Poetry Journal* and *Narrative*. Her collection, *Night Ladder* published by Glass Lyre Press in 2017 was a finalist for the Julie Suk Award and the Lascaux Poetry Prize for a poetry collection.

**Mark Tardi** – Mark Tardi is originally from Chicago and he earned his MFA from Brown University. His is the author of three books: *The Circus of Trust, Airport Music*, and *Euclid Shudders*. He has guest-edited and translated selections of contemporary Polish poetry for *Berlin Quarterly, Seedings*, and *Aufgabe*; and his poems have appeared on the Poetry Foundation website and in journals such as *Berkeley Poetry Review, Jet Fuel Review, textsound* and *Tammy*. A former Fulbright scholar, he lives with his family and two dogs in a village in central Poland and is on faculty at the University of Łód .

**Amy Gerstler** – Amy Gerstler's books of poems include *Scattered at Sea*, (Penguin, 2015), which was a finalist for the National Book Award, and *Dearest Creature* (Penguin, 2009) which was named a New York Times Book Review Notable Book, and was short listed for the Los Angeles Times Book Prize in Poetry. Her previous twelve books include *Ghost Girl, Medicine, Crown of Weeds, Nerve Storm*, and *Bitter Angel*, which won a National Book Critics Circle Award in poetry. She has received a Guggenheim Fellowship and a C.D. Wright Award from the Foundation for Contemporary Arts.

## PART III ESSAY: The Moral Lessons of the Holocaust (an ethical perspective)

**Mehnaz Afridi** – Mehnaz Afridi is Adjunct Professor at Gratz College and Associate Professor of Religious studies and Director of Holocaust, Genocide, and Interfaith Education Center at Manhattan College. She teaches Islam, Holocaust, Genocide and issues of gender within Islam. Her articles have appeared in books such as; *Sacred Tropes: Tanakh, New Testament, and Qur'an as Literature and Culture*, (Brill, 2006). *Not Your Father's Anti-Semitism: Hatred of the Jews in the 21st Century* (Paragon House, 2008). "A Muslim's Response to Frank H. Littel" in *Legacy of an Impassioned Plea Franklin H. Littel's Crucifixion of the Jews*, Ed. David Patterson, (New York: Paragon Press); "Muslim Memory and Righting Relations with the Other" in *Righting Relations After the Holocaust*, Eds. Elena G. Procario-Foley and Robert A. Cathey, (New Jersey: Paulist Press). "The Role of Muslims and the Holocaust" in Oxford Handbooks Online, (Oxford University Press, 2015). She is the co-editor of a book entitled *Orhan Pamuk and Global Literature: Existentialism and Politics* (May 2012, Palgrave Macmillan), and her book *Shoah through Muslim Eyes* (Academic Studies Press, 2017) was nominated for the Yad Vashem International Book Prize for Holocaust Research and the Jacob Schnitzer Book Award. Dr. Afridi obtained her PhD from University of South Africa, her MA and BA from Syracuse University.

## PART IV: Aftermath

**Linda Pastan** – A former Poet Laureate of Maryland, Linda Pastan (1932-2023) graduated from Radcliffe College, received an MA from Brandeis University and an honorary doctorate from Kenyon College. She published 15 volumes of poetry, most recently *Almost an Elegy: New and Later Selected Poems*. Two of these books have been finalists for the National Book Award. She won numerous awards, including The Radcliffe Distinguished Alumni Award and The Maurice English Award. In 2003 she won the Ruth Lilly Poetry Prize for lifetime achievement.

**Jean Nordhaus** – Jean Nordhaus' volumes of poetry include *Memos from the Broken World, Innocence,* and *The Porcelain Apes of Moses Mendelssohn.* She has published work in *American Poetry Review, the New Republic, Poetry* and *Best American Poetry* 2000 and 2007. Her work was featured in Innisfree Poetry Journal's "A Closer Look," and was a featured poet on the poetry-magazine.com website for the first half of 2019. In the past, she has served as poetry coordinator at the Folger Shakespeare Library, President of Washington Writers' Publishing House, and Review Editor of Poet Lore, the oldest continuously published poetry magazine in the U.S.

**Myra Sklarew** – Myra Sklarew, professor emerita, American University and former president, Yaddo Artists Community, is the author of collections of poetry, fiction and essays including *From the Backyard of the Diaspora* (National Jewish Book Council Award in Poetry); *Lithuania: New & Selected Poems* (Anna Davidson Rosenberg Award from the Judah Magnes Museum); *Over the Rooftops of Time: Jewish Essays, Stories and Poems* (SUNY Press) and *A Survivor Named Trauma: Holocaust Memory in Lithuania* (SUNY Press).

**M. Miriam Herrera** – M. Miriam Herrera is the poetry editor for *HaLapid: the Journal of the Society for Crypto Judaic Studies.* She is the author of the poetry collection, *Kaddish for Columbus,* published by Finishing Line Press. She is a graduate of the Program for Writers at the University of Illinois at Chicago. Her poems have appeared in *Earth's Daughters, New Millennium Writings, Blue Mesa Review, Nimrod, Southwestern American Literature, HaLapid,* and other journals. Herrera's parents are natives of the Rio Grande Valley of South Texas and are descended from Sefarditos—conversos or crypto-Jews who came to the new world to escape the Spanish Inquisition. She teaches writing and Mexican American Studies at the University of Texas Rio Grande Valley.

**Patty Seyburn** – Patty Seyburn is a professor at California State University, Long Beach. Her previous books are *Perfecta* (What Books Press, 2014), *Hilarity* (New Issues Press, 2009), *Mechanical Cluster* (Ohio State University Press, 2002) and *Diasporadic* (Helicon Nine Editions, 1998). She grew up in Detroit and holds degrees from Northwestern University, University of California, Irvine, and University of Houston. Her latest collection is *Threshold Delivery* (Finishing Line Press, 2019). She lives in Southern California with her husband, Eric, and two children, Sydney and Will.

**Gili Haimovich** – Gili Haimovich is a prizewinning bilingual poet in Hebrew and English. She won the international Italian poetry competition *Ossi di Seppia* for best foreign poet (2019) and awarded as outstanding artist by the Ministry of Culture, (Israel, 2015) among other nominations. Both her books in Hebrew *Landing Lights*, (2017) and *Baby Girl*, (2014) won grants from *The Acum Association of Authors* and her book *Reflected Like Joy*, (2002) won *The Pais Grant for Culture*. She is the author of the poetry book *Promised Lands* (2020) and two short collections: *Sideways Roots* (2017), and *Living on a Blank Page* (2008) written originally in English, six volumes of poetry in Hebrew, and a multi lingual book, *Note* (2019). Her poems have been translated into sixteen languages including English, French, Italian, Chinese and Serbian and are published worldwide in numerous journals and anthologies.

**Scott Nadelson** – Scott Nadelson is the author of a novel, a memoir, and six story collections, including *While It Lasts: Stories* winner of the Donald L. Jordan Prize for Literary Excellence and *One of Us*, winner of the G. S. Sharat Chandra Prize for Short Fiction, and *The Fourth Corner of the World*, named a Fiction Prize Honor Book by the Association of Jewish Libraries. He teaches at Willamette University and in the Rainier Writing Workshop MFA Program at Pacific Lutheran University. His work has appeared in a variety of magazines and literary journals, including *Ploughshares, The Southern Review, New England Review, Harvard Review, Glimmer Train*, and *Crazyhorse*, and his work has been cited as distinguished in both the *Best American Short Stories* and *Best American Essays* anthologies. He teaches at Willamette University, where he is Hallie Brown Ford Chair in Writing, and in the Rainier Writing Workshop MFA Program at Pacific Lutheran University.

**Barry Seiler** – Barry Seiler has published four books of poetry, three of them by University of Akron Press. *Frozen Falls*, the most recent, was a finalist for the Paterson Poetry Prize. He has received fellowships from the New York Foundation for the Arts and the New Jersey State Council on the Arts. The NJ State Council named him a Distinguished Artist in Poetry. He lives in Roxbury, a small town in the northern Catskills, with his wife Dian and three cats.

**Nomi Stone** – Nomi Stone is a poet and an anthropologist, and author of the poetry collections *Stranger's Notebook* (TriQuarterly 2008) and *Kill Class* (Tupelo 2019). Winner of a Pushcart Prize, Stone's poems appear in *POETRY* Magazine, *American Poetry Review, The New Republic, The Best American Poetry, Tin House, New England Review*, and elsewhere. *Kill Class* is based on two years of fieldwork she conducted within war trainings in mock Middle Eastern villages erected by the US military across America. Stone has an MFA in Poetry from Warren Wilson College and teaches at The University of Texas at Dallas.

**Saul Hillel Benjamin** – Saul Hillel Benjamin is late to fatherhood, earlier to poetry; earlier still to public service. Five years upper reaches of the first Clinton Administration; seven years in conflict resolution and school innovation work in Lebanon and Bosnia and Morocco. Fourteen years leading multicultural and "Great Books" interdisciplinary programs for high schools and universities in USA and Morocco. Published in *The American Scholar, The Yale Review, BBC-Three, The Christian Science Monitor, Dissent, The American Oxonian*, The Poetry Society of Great Britain, FM 107 Winnipeg, The 2019 San Diego Poetry Anthology, and chosen by a U.S. Poet Laureate and a UK Poet Laureate for the 2016 and 2017 Vice Chancellors International Poetry Anthologies.

**Richard Michelson** – Richard Michelson's many books for children, teens and adults have been listed among the Ten Best of the Year by *The New York Times, Publishers Weekly, The New Yorker*; and among the Best Dozen of the Decade by Amazon. Michelson received the 2017 National Jewish Book Award and the 2018 Sydney Taylor Gold Medal (his second) from the Association of Jewish Libraries. The Massachusetts Cultural Council awarded Michelson a 2016 Fellowship for his poetry collection *More Money than God* and his poems/essays have appeared in *Tikkun, Moment, Tablet* and elsewhere. His most recent poetry collection is *Sleeping as Fast as I Can* (Slant Books, 2023). Michelson served two terms as Poet Laureate in Northampton MA.

**Lia Pripstein** – Lia Pripstein was born in the Soviet Union and raised in Israel. She has worked as an educator, leading adult and teen workshops on the Holocaust and Jewish identity and interviewing Holocaust survivors for Steven Spielberg's SHOAH foundation. Her work has appeared in literary publications in Russian and in English language publications including *JewishFiction.net, Bacopa Literary Review* and on NPR. She lives in New York with her husband and two daughters, She has recently completed a political thriller set against the backdrop of the Israeli-Palestinian conflict.

## PART IV ESSAY: Living Responsibly after Auschwitz
## (an existential perspective)

**Sam Fleischacker** – Sam Fleischacker is LAS Distinguished Professor of Philosophy at the University of Illinois in Chicago (UIC), Director of Jewish Studies there, and founder of UIC's Jewish-Muslim Initiative. He works on moral and political philosophy, and the philosophy of religion. He is the author of eight books, including *The Good and the Good Book* (Oxford, 2015) and *Divine Teaching and the Way of the World*, (Oxford, 2011), both of which deal with the importance of revelation to our ethical lives, and he is the editor of two collections of papers, including *Heidegger's Jewish Followers* (Duquesne, 2008). His latest book is, *Being Me Being You: Adam Smith and Empathy* (University of Chicago Press, 2019).

# About the Editors

**Howard Debs** is a recipient of the 2015 Anna Davidson Rosenberg Poetry Awards. His book *Gallery: A Collection of Pictures and Words* is the recipient of a 2017 Best Book Award and 2018 Book Excellence Award. His chapbook *Political* is the 2021 American Writing Awards winner in poetry.

**Matthew Silverman** (M.E. Silverman) is co-editor of *The Bloomsbury Anthology of Contemporary American Jewish Poetry* and *101 Jewish Poems for the Third Millennium*, and author of *The Floating Door* and *The Breath Before Birds Fly*.

# About the NewVoicesProject

Instead of dealing with the Holocaust as a static historical event, and only a Jewish tragedy, the NewVoicesProject advocates a more dynamic approach with a focus on the moral lessons for all of humanity. The NewVoicesProject recognizes the international growth of xenophobia, threats to democracy, and the challenge of alternative truth enabled by social media. The NewVoicesProject involves a number of underwritten elements all designed to enhance Holocaust awareness and education, combining history lesson and inquiry into humanity's inhumanity through the arts. For more information visit https://newvoicesproject.org/

# Acknowledgments

The book *New Voices* is the anchor component of the broader NewVoicesProject dedicated to Holocaust awareness and education. Some six years of development has brought us to this result, only with the efforts and commitment of many. First, thanks to our publisher Vallentine Mitchell, publisher of the first English language edition of Anne Frank's diary; under the guidance of Stewart Cass they have steadfastly partnered with us, in consonance with the motivation to make a difference adhered to by his late father Frank Cass.

We have to thank all the contributors for going above and beyond the usual, and of course for the quality of their work; there was not much conventional in this undertaking, each poet and fiction writer having been selected and matched with a particular visual and asked to confront the past for the sake of the future, and in the case of our essayists, to render insight to help ensure the future.

Some contributors are also general advisors for the book and the overall project. We owe a special thanks to Mehnaz Afridi, Paul Vincent, and Joy Ladin in this regard, for guiding the vision all involved with the project share.

We must thank those who gave unstintingly of their expertise and experience; editorial consultants Emily Jo Scalzo and Robbi Nester, visuals consultant Maia Sutnik, print production consultant Shauna Makrealeas, media consultant John Brantingham, and marketing consultant Blaine Greenfield.

We want to acknowledge the significance of the contributions of artists Amy E. Bartell and Rachel Futterman who helped us visualize that which is beyond words.

We also want to acknowledge the assistance of the United States Holocaust Memorial Museum and in particular Caroline Waddell, photo archivist who was so very helpful with regard to the all-important photographs we needed after our long and arduous searching and selection.

Last but not least we want to thank our families including our respective spouses, children, grandchildren for all their support and encouragement as we pursued this project we considered of paramount importance; as the NewVoicesProject espouses, there is much at stake, we are in this together as human beings.

# Photo Credits

The NewVoicesProject has employed due diligence in seeking to identify copyright holders of the materials used in this compilation. We invite any copyright owners who are not properly identified to contact us at info@newvoicesproject.org. Some images have been marginally cropped to accommodate page layout requirements.

United States Holocaust Memorial Museum: pages 35, 37, 43, 45, 51, 54, 58, 60, 64, 66, 68, 70, 79, 83, 85, 88, 101, 104, 109, 111, 115, 117, 129, 132, 134, 136, 146, 150, 153, 157, 159, 163, 175, 176, 178, 185, 195, 200, 204.

CTK Photobank: page 41

Getty Images: page 106; Bettmann Collection via Getty Images

Yad Vashem: pages 139, 141, 143, 155, 166, 190 (Photo Archive, Jerusalem)

American Jewish Joint Distribution Committee: pages 181, 183 (JDC Archives)

bpk Bildagentur / Art Resource, NY: page 62

UN Photo Library: page 206 (UN Photo/MB)

Bundesarchiv: pages 119, 121 (Bild 183-H25217, 146-1975-041-07/unknown)

Hamburg Institute for Social Research: pages 81, 113

Bayerische Staatsbibliothek (Bavarian State Library): page 47

The Image Works: page 56 ©Roger-Viollet [license by The Image Works]

Israel Government Press Office: page 197 (Hans Pin, photographer)

The NewVoicesProject wishes to acknowledge all those who through their philanthropic support further the NewVoicesProject mission to focus on the moral lessons of the Holocaust through the arts, and particularly recognize the donations of the following who made *New Voices* possible:

Marilyn Samwick, in memory of grandparents
Anna and David Brin, Bertha and Morris Kessler

Meryl and Harvey Strackman in memory of our parents
Edith and Philip Levine, Minnie and Sam Strackman

The Mogen Foundation

Ingram Content Group UK Ltd.
Milton Keynes UK
UKHW011819280323
419313UK00001B/16